PROTAGORAS

PLATO

PROTAGORAS

Translated, with Notes, by

Stanley Lombardo

&

Karen Bell

Introduced by

Michael Frede

Hackett Publishing Company
Indianapolis & Cambridge

Plato: ca. 428–347 B.C.

The translators have gratefully incorporated in this third printing a few revisions proposed by John Cooper during his preparation of *The Complete Works of Plato* (Hackett, 1997) in which our translation of the *Protagoras* appears.

Cover design by Listenberger Design & Associates

Interior design by Dan Kirklin

For further information, please address

Hackett Publishing Company, Inc.
P.O. Box 44937
Indianapolis, Indiana 46244-0937

Library of Congress Cataloging-in-Publication Data

Plato.
 [Protagoras. English]
 Protagoras/Plato; translated, with notes, by Stanley Lombardo & Karen Bell; introduced by Michael Frede.
   p. cm.
 Translation of: Protagoras.
 Includes bibliographical references.
 ISBN 0-87220-095-7 (hard: alk. paper):
 ISBN 0-87220-094-9 (pbk.: alk. paper)
 1. Protagoras. 2. Socrates. 3. Sophists (Greek philosophy)
4. Ethics. I. Lombardo, Stanley, 1943–   II. Bell, Karen, 1950–
III. Title.
B382.A5T3913 1991
170—dc20   91-28322
                   CIP

CONTENTS

ACKNOWLEDGMENTS

We acknowledge Hackett's anonymous readers for their careful reading of the manuscript.

Stanley Lombardo wishes to thank the University of Kansas for supporting work on this translation through a sabbatical leave and its General Research Fund.

Karen Bell wishes to thank California State University, Fresno, Department of Philosophy, the University Research Committee, the Affirmative Action Faculty Development Fund, and the Dean of the School of Arts and Humanities for their generous support of this translation.

INTRODUCTION

Michael Frede

(I) The Place of the Protagoras in Moral Thought

The core of Plato's *Protagoras* is a purported discussion between Socrates and Protagoras concerning virtue. Toward the end of the dialogue, Socrates is made to say: "I have no other reason for asking these things than my desire to answer these questions about virtue, especially what virtue is in itself" (360e6–8). Some lines later, he is made to explain this concern: "Since I take . . . forethought over my life as a whole, I pay attention to these things . . ." (361d3–5).

As we shall see, the Socrates of the dialogue suggests a particular position, according to which one's entire life depends on the view one takes of what virtue is and of what is true about virtue. He thinks that if one has the wrong views one's life is bound to be a failure; if one has the right views one's life is bound to be a success—hence the urgency with which he pursues these questions. Even if we do not share this view, its discussion in the dialogue remains interesting for at least two reasons. Even if the connection between one's life and one's views about virtue is not as straightforward as Socrates takes it to be, there is a connection that makes the questions the dialogue raises vital ones, questions that affect our lives profoundly. It does make a difference to our lives what, in the end, we want to have succeeded in; it makes a difference what we

John Cooper, as so often before, generously helped me with many detailed comments and queries. But I am particularly grateful to Paul Coppock, who took it upon himself to thoroughly revise my draft. It thereby gained greatly in clarity of exposition.

think it takes on our part to succeed, what abilities and kinds of competence we think we need in order to be, as we say nowadays, competent human beings; we want to know what it would take to be the kind of person one would, on reflection, like to be, if that were possible; whether and how one could acquire this ability and competence, and what roles natural endowment, upbringing, and reflection play in this. It makes a difference to what extent we think a society requires and is entitled to insist on, by coercion if necessary, a certain level of competence in living our lives; and whether we think that in order to succeed we need some critical knowledge to rectify the systematically distorted beliefs that life in a society tends to induce and which, if we lacked this knowledge, would guide us in our preferences. These questions, and others like them, are forcefully raised by the discussion in the *Protagoras*.

Second, not only do the answers to these questions have an obvious bearing on our lives; our own thought on these questions, however inarticulate and conventional it may be, has itself been shaped by a long tradition, in which reflection on the position and the questions Socrates invites us to consider play a major role. Plato's moral thinking in the middle and the later dialogues (cf. e.g. *Republic* 435e ff.; *Philebus* 20c ff.) is crucially shaped by his highly qualified acceptance of the suggestion, made by Socrates in this early dialogue, that the good life is a matter of knowing what is good; and so will be Aristotle's moral philosophy, though his acceptance is even more qualified (cf. e.g. *E.N.* 1145b21 ff.). When the Stoics reject these qualifications, to return to what they take to be the unqualified, undiluted, uncompromising doctrine of Socrates, they seem to obtain this doctrine in good part from an interpretation of our dialogue. At least, this seems the easiest explanation of a surprising number of parallels between views put forward by Socrates in the *Protagoras* and Stoic doctrine.[1] Similarly, when, in the *Nicomachean Ethics*, Aristotle discusses Socrates' view on weakness of the will, his language clearly shows that he relies on the exposition of this view in the *Protagoras* (cf. *E.N.* 1145b23 ff. and *Prot.* 352b–c).

---

1. For example in their views on the "passions of the soul," "weakness of the will," the "unity" of the virtues, and on reason as the governing part, the *hegemonikon* (cf. 352b4)—quite apart from the identification of virtue with wisdom, of wisdom with knowledge of the good, and the assumption that virtue is a necessary, but also sufficient, condition for the good life.

Philosophers in late antiquity, it is true, had little interest in the *Protagoras*. Its undogmatic and unspeculative character did not appeal to a time which was looking for salvation in dogma, sometimes even in dogma beyond the reach of reason. Although it contains certain claims that almost ask to be expanded and developed in the context of some larger theory, still, like the other early dialogues and unlike the middle ones, the *Protagoras* proceeds rather untheoretically; and even when it seems to suggest certain views, their tentative and provisional character is emphasized. One is not even tempted to accept any of these views without further reflection or inquiry.

At the beginning of the nineteenth century, however, when Plato again came to be more widely read, and even more when, later in that century, he became an important part of any higher education, the *Protagoras* regained a great appeal, in particular to the reform-minded. John Stuart Mill, for instance, devoted to the *Protagoras* the first of a series of essays on Platonic dialogues in the *Monthly Repository* (VIII, 1834, pp. 89–99 and 203–211; Collected Works, vol. xi, p. 39 ff.). He was attracted to it, at a time when, as he complains, Plato was sadly neglected, not only because of the dialogue's sympathetic characterization of the sophists, for whom he shared Grote's[2] admiration, but because he saw in the *Protagoras* a precursor of his own utilitarianism.

So the *Protagoras* plays an important role in the tradition of moral thought; and thus, at least indirectly, it has had an impact on how we have come to think about these questions, which, in some version or other, still matter to us as much as they did to Plato and his contemporaries.

(II) The Athenian Background of the Debate about Virtue

Let us turn to the details of the dialogue. As we noted, toward the end of the dialogue Socrates says it is a concern for his life that makes him pursue these questions about virtue (361d4–5). This pursuit is not an idle intellectual pastime, nor does it take place in a vacuum. What gives the dialogue its power, what draws us in and engages us, is in good part the art with which Plato fills out the context in which the argument is set forth.

---

2. Cf. Grote's influential *History of Greece* (London, 1846) and his *Plato and the Other Companions of Sokrates* (London, 1865), both of which Mill reviewed.

The *Protagoras* is striking not just for the length, complexity, and richness of the argument, but also for the unusually rich and lively detail of its setting.

To begin with the external form of the dialogue, it has a double frame: Socrates meets a friend who asks him whether he has just come from seeing Alcibiades. The ensuing conversation between Socrates and his friend is the first frame. Socrates has just seen Alcibiades, he says, but paid no attention to him, because they were in the company of somebody far more attractive than Alcibiades, because wiser, namely Protagoras. Socrates is very cautious, though, not to commit himself to the assumption that Protagoras, in fact, is wise (cf. 309c10; d1–2). In this way we are introduced to two central topics of the dialogue: the supreme attractiveness of wisdom and the question of what constitutes wisdom. Asked by his friend for an account of the meeting with the famous sophist, Socrates starts out by explaining how he came to have a discussion with Protagoras (310e8 ff.). Hippocrates, a young acquaintance of his, has heard that Protagoras is in town, and wants Socrates to help him persuade Protagoras to take him on as a student (310e2–3). Socrates' report of his conversation with Hippocrates constitutes the second frame.

Hippocrates obviously comes from a well-to-do family and wants to succeed in life, more particularly in public life (cf. 316b10–c1). However, he does not want to rely solely on what we may presume to be his good traditional upbringing. He wants to acquire the wisdom Protagoras is supposed to have and impart to his students (310d5–6; cf. 318e4–5). This suggests that Protagoras' wisdom is an art or expertise that he can impart by teaching. But the ensuing discussion between Hippocrates and Socrates shows that Hippocrates is quite confused, both about the nature of the wisdom Protagoras imparts and about how it might benefit or harm him. So the discussion with Protagoras, once Socrates and Hippocrates gain admittance to the sophist's presence, will begin with the question what it is precisely that Protagoras promises to teach.

As they are about to enter Callias' house, where Protagoras is staying, Socrates and Hippocrates pause at the door to finish the discussion they had continued on their way; the doorman obviously overhears them; so when they knock, he opens and says, "Ha! More sophists! He's busy," and slams the door in their faces. When they finally gain entrance, they see

Protagoras walking in the portico flanked by two groups. On one side were Hipponicus and his brother on his mother's side, Paralus, son of Pericles, and Charmides, son of Glaucon. On the other side were Pericles' other son, Xanthippus, Philippides, son of Philomelus, and Antimoerus of Mendes, Protagoras' star pupil who is studying professionally to become a sophist. Following behind and trying to listen to what was being said were a group of what seemed to be mostly foreigners, men whom Protagoras collects from the various cities he travels through. He enchants them with his voice like Orpheus, and they follow the sound of his voice in a trance. There were some locals also in this chorus, whose dance simply delighted me when I saw how beautifully they took care never to get in Protagoras' way. When he turned around with his flanking groups, the audience to the rear would split into two in a very orderly way and then circle around to either side and form up again behind him. It was quite lovely. (314e3–315b8)

In addition to those mentioned in this passage we also learn that the following are present: the sophists Hippias and Prodicus, Plato's relative Critias, who also appears in the dialogue *Charmides*; Phaedrus, Pausanias, Alcibiades, Eryximachus, and the playwright Agathon, all of whom appear in the dialogue *Symposium*, the Andron who also is mentioned in the *Gorgias* (487c), Adeimantus, a general in the Peloponnesian War, and another Adeimantus. Present, then, are the major sophists (only Gorgias is missing), six persons after whom a Platonic dialogue is named, for the most part persons who turn up once or more in Plato's dialogues outside the *Protagoras*, some of Plato's relatives, sons of some of the most prominent Athenian families, some men who over the next thirty years will play a prominent or even fateful, but in any case questionable, role in Athenian history. At least four of those present (Alcibiades, Eryximachus, Phaedrus, and Adeimantus) will be implicated in the scandal of the sacrilegious mutilation of Hermae in 415 B.C., which will lead to the recall of Alcibiades as one of the commanders of the Sicilian expedition, his condemnation, and his temporarily changing sides in the war with Sparta. One, Andron, a friend of

Callicles, will be a member of the oligarchical regime of the so-called Four Hundred in 411 B.C. and two, Critias and Charmides, both relatives of Plato, will form part of the so-called tyranny of the Thirty in 404 B.C. What are we to make of this? Why do the sophists and in particular Protagoras attract promising young men with such force? Part of the attraction, no doubt, is that Protagoras is supposed to be a powerful speaker (cf. 310e6–7), and they hope the sophist will turn them, too, into powerful speakers (cf. 312d6–7; d9). In a democratic society that does not acknowledge any rights of the individual and in which most important decisions are made by the people, a large assembly, or a court with a large jury, on the basis of speeches, the ability to speak well is, no doubt, a crucial and perhaps vital asset for young men of ambition. But we need not underestimate the young men we encounter here by supposing they are just out to make a career in public life. Rather, they seem somehow aware that a traditional education is insufficient to deal with the problems a citizen of Athens faces in the second half of the fifth century. They sense that traditional ways are inadequate, that one must approach problems in an enlightened, rational way, and that there should be a special competence, an expertise, in dealing with them. Indeed, according to the dialogue, Protagoras promises to impart just such an expertise. He is made to say that he will teach his students precisely what they come for, and he explains that he teaches how best to run one's household, sound deliberation in one's own affairs, but also in the affairs of the city, and how one is best able to act and speak concerning them (318e4 ff.). He is ready to accept Socrates' suggestion that he teaches the *politike techne* (319a4). Often this is translated as "the art of politics," but, from the context, what Protagoras has in mind is perhaps rather the art of the citizen, the competence that makes a citizen a good citizen (cf. 319a4–5), part of which is to run one's household properly (318e5–6).

Now, one can immediately see why such a claim, on the part of an influential and respected figure like Protagoras, would be regarded as a threat by the people, by democrats. Democracy rests on the assumption that the affairs of a city are not the subject of some special expertise, but that every citizen is competent to judge them. To claim that a special expertise or art is needed for these matters comes dangerously close to claiming that the people are not fit to rule, for they do not have this expertise. They may not have the talent to acquire it. They certainly do not have the time or the money to enroll with Protagoras. The fact that Protagoras attracts ambitious young men, from prominent families, whose attitude towards democracy is ambivalent, would heighten the misgivings. On the other hand, he does not attack democratic procedures, and seems unwilling to. On the contrary, he rhetorically supports the ideology on which these procedures rest. The result is a certain confusion in his own position: he supports the value of special expertise, but also the democratic ethos that is fundamentally at odds with it.

Protagoras' confusion manifests itself in a certain ambiguity in his claim to teach good citizenship. Truly virtuous action has to satisfy at least two conditions: (i) it must be an action of the right kind, and (ii) it must spring from the appropriate motivation. Not only must it be a good thing to do, but it must also be done out of goodness, out of a settled and enduring attitude, a certain disposition of mind or character or both. This seems to be the point of the contrast between "becoming good" and "being good," drawn by Socrates in his interpretation of Simonides' poem (339e6 ff.), a passage whose seeming irrelevance to the subject at issue has troubled interpreters. Socrates interprets Simonides as claiming that it is difficult enough to "become good," but impossible to be good, at least for a human being. The curious phrase "becoming good," as we can see from, for example, its repeated use in Thucydides (II, 87, 9; III, 64, 2 and 4; VII, 77, 7), refers to the kind of behavior a virtuous person would display, where it is left open, or even questioned, whether in the case at hand it actually is produced by virtue. When, in his speech (320c ff.), Protagoras claims that, and explains how, all Athenians teach virtue, what he largely seems to have in mind is a kind of conditioning which, by threat or lure, manages to make people, by and large, exhibit the kind of behavior thought desirable. But this, at best, constitutes "becoming good," rather than being good. Being good is a matter of acting freely out of insight, and not out of social coercion.

The difference, in a way, is the difference between vulgar or popular virtue, which amounts to behaving as "good citizens" are supposed to behave, and real virtue, which is a matter of personal attitude determined by insight, a difference Plato refers to in the *Phaedo* (82a10 ff.) and the *Republic* (619c7 ff.). This, then, is the ambiguity in Protagoras' position: When he claims to teach good citizenship, is it real or popular virtue he has in mind? That he conceives of it as some kind of wisdom suggests he is talking about real virtue. But the way he talks about virtue and its inculcation makes him seem rather to be an advocate of popular virtue. His skill can perhaps make popular virtue more attractive, and he may refine and enhance it; but it is not real virtue and not the kind of thing that can be taught, at least not in the same sense as an art or a science.

Socrates, on the other hand, seems to think that virtue is wisdom; and, given his view of the difficulty of attaining knowledge, he must, like Simonides on his interpretation, think that it is next to impossible to be virtuous. True virtue is not just somehow managing to behave, or having somehow been pushed, perhaps by rhetoric like Protagoras', into behaving as we would like people to behave. One must oneself come to understand, and hence to accept, how it is good to behave, as if it had become one's nature to behave well. For Socrates, virtue is crucially a matter of motivation, more precisely of understanding and wisdom. Further, given that, as we shall see, he believes that such understanding cannot be overridden or set aside by any other motive, he thinks that virtue is *entirely* a matter of wisdom. Needless to say, he will hardly agree with Protagoras that wisdom is widely distributed among his fellow-Athenians, or that it is successfully taught by them.

There is an irony in all this which can hardly escape the reader and surely is intended. Socrates presents himself as less wise than Protagoras, who, with his cautious prudence and respect for traditional values and democratic views, manages to avoid harm (cf. e.g. 316c–317c), but also has become quite confused in his own position; and it will be Socrates who will pay with his life for his own consistency and lack of prudence. The Athenians, their democracy regained, will put him to death in 399 B.C. The reaction of the doorman who had listened to the end of Socrates' discussion with Hippocrates is telling: it is meant to indicate that the people found it quite difficult to distinguish between Socrates and the sophists. Socrates is very interested in, and on good terms with, sophists like Protagoras and Prodicus. He draws on the same questionable following of young men as the sophists; and he, like Protagoras, questions the adequacy of their traditional upbringing and envisages a rational art or discipline to guide one's life, private or public. But, unlike Protagoras, Socrates uncompromisingly insists on the idea of a special expertise, in spite of its obvious consequences for our attitude both towards traditional values and democratic tenets.

(III) The Nature of Dialectic

One important part of the background of the dialogue, then, is the social and political situation of Athens, which is about to embark on an imperialist war that will end in complete disaster. Another is the character of the protagonists, which is sketched in considerable detail. Protagoras' caution and prudence, his desire to be respectable, and his decency are clearly connected with his views and the way he argues, just as Socrates' views and the way he argues are connected with his fate. Thus the dialogue represents dramatically how the issues in question are embedded in our lives, which shape our answers to them and which in turn are shaped by these answers. Indeed, also important in the background of the dialogue are the very styles of thought and argument represented by Protagoras and Socrates. Though Protagoras is also famed for his succinct answers in debate (cf. 334e6 ff.), his strength obviously is in carefully crafting speeches that overwhelm the audience as if by magic. The dialogue, at 320c8 ff., presents a powerful example of such a speech and its effects. Perhaps it is a testimony to Plato's literary abilities that scholars have seriously considered whether the speech in some sense can be attributed to the historical Protagoras. Socrates, on the other hand, proceeds "dialectically," by short question and answer, so that we can see precisely on what assumptions and inferential steps a given conclusion rests, instead of being carried away by the magic of a speech. Our dialogue, however, shows that this style of argument was not peculiar to Socrates, but characteristic of a more general practice, cultivated also by the sophists, which was familiar to the audience and conducted according to certain agreed-upon rules (cf., e.g., 335a4 ff.; 338a8 ff.). Indeed, the *Protagoras* is perhaps our most important source of knowledge about this practice, a source which has not yet been sufficiently explored.

This manner of arguing by question and answer, in which Socrates obviously developed great skill, gives Plato's dialogues their basic form. This accounts for the fact that the dialogues do not portray what we would think of as real discussions—full exchanges of views. Rather, the dialogues follow the rules of dialectic. There is a questioner and a respondent. The questioner elicits from the respondent a thesis, and the task of the questioner is to compel, by the appropriate use of yes-or-no questions, admissions from the respondent that contradict his original thesis. It is part of the formal role of the respondent in dialectic that he answers just with "yes" or "no." This does not make for much of a discussion in our sense, and it certainly constrains the respondent, a feature unfairly exploited by some sophisms, like the argument which asks, "Have you stopped beating your wife?" The *Protagoras* gives us a vivid picture of the practice of dialectic, of how the respondent can be fair or unfair, cooperative or uncooperative, of how the questioner can conceal the aim of his questioning, of the role the audience plays, of the possible need for an umpire (cf. 338a8). But our dialogue also allows Protagoras, the main character besides Socrates, repeatedly to break this scheme; for example, to exchange roles with Socrates (338e6 ff.), or to hold forth in long speeches. For this reason, the form of the dialogue in the *Protagoras* is much more varied than in most dialogues of Plato.

Now, one particular feature of dialectic, as practiced by Socrates, needs brief comment. To win in this kind of debate is to force the respondent to contradict something he had originally claimed. Originally he had claimed that *p*, and now he is forced to admit that not *p*. This practice fits Socrates' purposes admirably. Socrates always claims ignorance and is, to say the least, hesitant to state his own views (cf. *Apology* 20e6 ff.; *Theaetetus* 149a ff.). He wants to hear what others have to say, and he wants to determine whether they speak from knowledge or ignorance. Dialectic provides Socrates with an ideal means to show his interlocutors that, though they think they know, they are speaking out of ignorance. By contradicting himself on the very subject of his presumed competence, the opponent shows himself not to be much of an expert. Coming to acknowledge this ignorance, though painful, is the first necessary step toward real knowledge or wisdom. The argument, then, which forces the respondent to admit that not *p* need not really constitute a proof that not *p*. All it needs to show is that the respondent is prepared to make assumptions from which it would follow that not *p*; but these are not necessarily assumptions Socrates himself is making. After all, Socrates is just asking questions, and we can at best guess how he himself would answer them. The arguments do not so much refute a thesis or establish its contradictory, as they refute a person by showing him to be inconsistent and confused.

Socrates' mastery of this practice is such that he manages to "refute" the respondent even where we have some reason to believe that Socrates actually shares the respondent's view—which just goes to show that it is not the thesis, strictly speaking, but the respondent who is refuted. One gets the feeling that Socrates could manage to refute any thesis; that is, that he could show anyone to be ignorant on any of the questions at issue in such discussions. It is not clear which moral we should draw from this—that knowledge is indeed difficult to come by, or that, at least in fact, if not in principle, there is no knowledge. The Stoics drew the former moral, that it takes Herculean labors to gain the knowledge which constitutes wisdom, and that human beings in principle are capable of knowledge, though in fact as a rule are too weak to submit themselves to the toils. The Skeptics, equally inspired by Socrates, inclined to the view that even such Herculean labors, a life uncompromisingly devoted to philosophical inquiry, may not suffice to achieve this aim, though it might leave one in a state of Socratic ignorance, rather than the common state of pretense and pretension. What is clear, though, once we understand the nature of dialectic and the conception of knowledge for which Socrates' dialectical questioning is supposed to constitute a test, is that Socrates' own claims to ignorance are not disingenuous or sheer irony. Even when he seems to have a view on a matter and, moreover, a view which happens to coincide with that of the respondent, what really matters is that this is just a view, not supported by the kind of knowledge which would enable one to rationally hold on to it whatever considerations to the contrary might be available.

(IV) The Reversal

That a dialectical argument is sometimes meant to refute the respondent's claim to knowledge, rather than to show that his thesis is false, helps to explain the odd reversal of positions on which Socrates remarks near the end of the dialogue (361a3 ff.). In his eagerness to show that virtue is some one thing, Socrates has been arguing that virtue is some kind of knowledge, that virtue is wisdom. This would strongly suggest that virtue can be taught; but that is precisely what Protagoras had originally claimed and what Socrates had set out to argue against. Protagoras, on the other hand, in his eagerness to deny that the virtues are very much alike, if not identical, has taken the view that courage, for example, quite definitely is not a matter of knowledge or wisdom. By taking this position, however, he has committed himself to the view that virtue, or at least one of the virtues, not being a matter of knowledge, cannot be taught. At the beginning of the argument, however, although Protagoras has been cautious not to explicitly claim to teach virtue, he does not object when Socrates proceeds as if he had claimed that the wisdom, learning, or *mathema* he imparts to his students is in fact virtue (cf., e.g., 319a10–b1 and 320b4–c1). Nor is Socrates without reason to suppose that Protagoras thinks of himself as teaching virtue, since he agrees that his aim is to turn men into good citizens by teaching them the art of the citizen (319a4–7). At that point, then, it looks not only as if Protagoras thinks that virtue can be taught, but that it can be taught because it is a certain wisdom, and wisdom really is an art or expertise. In fact, using an old-fashioned synonym of "wisdom" (*euboulia*), Protagoras himself characterizes the learning he imparts as a matter of some kind of wisdom (318e5).

This not only sounds very much like the position generally associated with Socrates, but like the position towards which Socrates is arguing in this dialogue: that the virtues, and hence virtue, are wisdom and so can be taught. Given all this, we need to ask not only how the reversal of positions comes about, but, more fundamentally, why Socrates objects in the first place to Protagoras' claim that virtue can be taught, when, in fact, it appears he agrees with him to an amazing degree.

Here it is important to remember the dialectical and, in particular, elenctic character of Socrates' arguments; that is to say, Socrates' use of dialectical argument to test the expertise of the respondent and to reveal his ignorance and confusion, even though Socrates might well agree with his interlocutor's thesis. On the first page of the dialogue (309), Socrates already, by his careful language, indicates that he has reservations about Protagoras' wisdom. Though Protagoras claims his wisdom to be a *mathema*, an art (*techne*), Socrates politely doubts whether Protagoras has such a body of systematic knowledge to impart (319a8–9). And Socrates obviously has doubts concerning Protagoras' conception of virtue and how, given this conception, he can think of virtue as a *techne*. Consequently, when he finds out that his young friend Hippocrates is ready to turn himself over to Protagoras to become wiser and better, Socrates puts Protagoras to the test of a dialectical examination, for all to see whether he has the wisdom or knowledge he claims to impart. As the discussion evolves, it will also become clearer why Socrates was right to question Protagoras' wisdom. Protagoras' reversal of position is no dialectical strategy, but rather is rooted in the political cautiousness mentioned above and the confused conception of virtue that it motivates. Protagoras should hold on to the fundamental insight that virtue is a matter of wisdom and that wisdom is some expert knowledge, though this, perhaps, needs some qualification. But, instead of trying to get clearer about this, working out its consequences and systematically developing and articulating the relevant expertise, Protagoras hesitates to speak his mind and to develop his view in a direction which inevitably would bring him into conflict, not only with the people of Athens, but also with traditionalists among the upper class. Instead, as we have seen, he compromises his position, and this compromise leads to the reversal and to Protagoras' downfall.

When Socrates challenges the thesis that virtue can be taught and points out that at least the Athenians (cf. 319d3–4) do not seem to think that virtue is some special expertise (319b5 ff.) for which special teachers are needed (319d5–6), or that it can be taught at all (319d6–7), Protagoras is willing to defend the thesis at great length. He argues, among other things, that any civilized society treats virtue as a skill or competence which, in the division of labor, is not divided, because every citizen needs it, and thus society makes sure that everybody acquires it (cf., e.g., 322d1 ff.; 326e8–327a2). Hence every effort is made, both on the part of the society as a whole and of its individual members, to teach virtue to the young (cf., e.g., 326e2–4 and 327e1–3). Protagoras concludes his long speech (328c3 ff.) by claiming that he has shown that the Athenians, too, assume that virtue can be taught, and that, indeed, they are teaching it all the time.

This defense of the dangerous claim to teach virtue is politically expedient, since it provides a foundation for the democrats' claim that every citizen, because of his virtue, is entitled to the epithet "good," which the aristocrats had reserved for themselves, and thus has the competence to participate in the affairs of the city; but it compromises and confuses Protagoras' own position. The citizens have their own notion of virtue, and it is not the notion of a *techne*, some special expertise or knowledge, as Socrates seems to think and as Protagoras had originally seemed to suggest. In consequence, the citizens also have their own idea of how virtue is taught—namely, by traditional upbringing and education, which is largely accomplished by conditioning, often by some form of coercive persuasion, rather than by imparting or fostering rational, reflective insight, in the way Socrates and Protagoras originally seem to think.

Protagoras is aware of a certain tension in his position. The question naturally arises why, if all Athenians teach virtue and are reasonably successful at raising good citizens, there is any need for his services. In his long speech (328a3 ff.), he tries to address this problem by pointing out that his services should still be appreciated, since he is somewhat better able than others to advance his students' virtue beyond what their traditional education would achieve. Indeed, in hindsight, one may see some significance in the fact that Protagoras has been rather careful not to promise to make his students good or virtuous, but merely better every day (316c9 ff.; 318a9). This differential increase is well worth the fees he is charging, Protagoras points out at 328b3 ff.; he is catering to the promising, ambitious sons of the Athenian well-to-do, who traditionally, in their concern for virtue, do not spare their resources but send their sons to all kinds of teachers anyway (326b6–c6). But this defense of the need for his teaching only reflects the awkwardness of Protagoras' position, in spite of his praise of the citizens' virtue. It acknowledges, as the meeting in Callias' house also shows, that he is surrounded by ambitious sons of the well-to-do and of aristocratic families who, as their subsequent history shows, are hardly friends of the people and have a pronounced tendency to support oligarchic rule. He is easily seen, not as providing an increase in civic virtue welcome to everybody, but as giving the well-to-do the edge, an increase in competence which, in the best case, will justify their claim to power and, in the worst, will allow them to succeed in the pursuit of their self-interest by their incredible ability to handle arguments and to persuade, just as on this occasion Protagoras manages, by his long speech, to charm and cast a spell on his audience and so to persuade them that virtue can be taught.

(V) The Structure of the Central Argument

The formal situation in the dialogue at the conclusion of Protagoras' great speech is this. Protagoras has committed himself to the thesis that virtue can be taught. Socrates has challenged this thesis (319a10), but instead of immediately proceeding to "refute" it, Socrates gave Protagoras occasion to defend his claim in a long speech. It is in this situation, only at 329b7, that Socrates begins the long dialectical argument which forms the argumentative backbone of the dialogue, ending at 360e5. Even now, however, Socrates does not attack Protagoras' thesis directly. In fact, he talks as if he might be willing to let Protagoras get away with asserting the teachability of virtue. Rather, he seems to raise a new question. Relying on Protagoras' long speech, Socrates elicits from him the opinion that virtue consists of a number of virtues that are distinct and quite different from each other. Formally, this, rather than the teachability of virtue, is the thesis which Socrates sets out to refute, it seems successfully. But once this argument concerning the unity of virtue is concluded at 360e5, Socrates points out politely that it could easily have been extended to constitute a formal refutation of Protagoras' original thesis that virtue can be taught: as mentioned above, Protagoras seems to have committed himself, in the course of this argument concerning the unity of virtue, to the view that courage, at least, is not some kind of knowledge or expertise and hence cannot be taught. What is more, Socrates drives home the point that Protagoras has shown himself to be confused about what virtue is and hence does not know whether or not it can be taught. A fortiori, Protagoras cannot claim to be an expert on virtue and so is in no position to teach it. Hippocrates, obviously, should think twice before submitting himself to Protagoras' teaching. The argumentative core and backbone of the dialogue, then, consists of a long argument, repeatedly interrupted, concerning the unity of the virtues, or the unity of virtue, which extends from 329b7 to 360e5. Its great relevance to the question of the teachability of virtue, and to the more basic question of the nature of virtue itself, only gradually becomes more apparent in the course of the argument.

It is in 329c1 ff. that Socrates raises the question of the unity of virtue: "Is virtue a single thing with justice and temperance and piety its parts, or are the things I have just listed all names for a single entity?" On the face of it, there does not seem to be a problem here, and Socrates' question looks artificial. Protagoras is saying that there are different virtues, but that they go together so as to constitute one thing, namely virtue: "Virtue is a single thing," he replies, "and the things you are asking about are its parts."

In fact, Socrates' question is less artificial than it seems. Protagoras himself had suggested (318e5) that virtue is a certain kind of wisdom. If so, wisdom is not just one among several virtues. Rather, one must wonder whether wisdom is also a necessary condition for the other virtues or even whether the other virtues are not just parts of this wisdom. Perhaps, indeed, one and the same wisdom, applied in different contexts, grounds or even guarantees a courageous or pious or just response, as the context demands. In any case, as Protagoras' own words show, there is a serious question about how the virtues go together to form virtue. So Socrates quite naturally proceeds, in 329d4 ff. (cf. 349a6 ff.; 359a4 ff.), to ask more specifically how Protagoras thinks the different virtues are related to each other and to virtue itself so as to form one thing. The view he elicits from Protagoras is the following: The individual virtues are, first, quite distinct and unlike each other, and unlike the whole (virtue itself) of which they are parts. That is, they are un-homogeneous, like the parts of a face, which differ from each other and from the face itself; rather than homogeneous, like the parts of a single lump of gold, which are like each other and like the whole lump. Second, the individual virtues are mutually independent, in the sense that one can have one virtue without having the others (329e2 ff.). These rather abstract statements remain somewhat vague, but in any case, the claim that Socrates will subject to criticism is that the virtues are not identical, one and the same, with each other and with virtue, or even qualitatively similar to each other, but rather qualitatively different parts of one and the same thing, namely virtue (cf. the recapitulation in 349a6 ff. and 359a4 ff.).

To refute this thesis, it would suffice to show of any two virtues that they are like, and not unlike, each other; but Socrates does not content himself with this. In his Great Speech, and elsewhere, Protagoras has mentioned or accepted at least five virtues. Socrates takes up these five virtues in four pairs: (i) justice and piety, (ii) wisdom and temperance, (iii) temperance and justice, and (iv) wisdom and courage. He tries to show, for each of the four pairs, that the two virtues in question are not unlike each other. But Socrates does this in such a way as to suggest that the virtues not only are like each other, but that their relation is much closer, perhaps even that they are identical with each other and hence with virtue. Nevertheless, some of the conclusions concerning the pairs of virtues do not obviously amount to straightforward claims of identity. So the refutation of Protagoras' thesis seems to leave open a whole range of positive possibilities as to how the virtues go together to constitute virtue, including the possibility that the different virtue-names refer to a single state of the soul. Hence the problem of the unity of virtue is a problem of interpretation for the *Protagoras*, but it is also a philosophical problem which will occupy Plato, Aristotle, and the Stoics. And it is a problem which should also occupy us. For when we think about what kind of person we ideally would want to be like, we also have to ask ourselves whether the list of features we find desirable just constitutes, as it were, a shopping-list, or whether, as seems likely, they are systematically related so as to form some kind of unity which goes beyond their being severally desirable features. How do we make comparisons and judge people, if there are a number of different and perhaps even independent relevant features?

Perhaps it is misleading to say that in the case of the *Protagoras* it is a problem of interpretation. For this would suggest that the Socrates of the dialogue is committed—has been committed by Plato, in writing the dialogue—to a certain position on the question, and that the interpreter's task is to find out which position it is. Here we should keep in mind the nature of dialectic: Strictly speaking, Socrates, as the questioner in the debate, is not committed to a view anyway. By having Socrates put his questions and draw his conclusions in a way which raises, but does not settle, the question of the unity of the virtues, Plato may have made the point precisely to encourage us to pursue for ourselves the different possibilities.

This said, it still seems true that, if the dialogue does suggest a positive thesis, it is the strong thesis that the virtues are identical with wisdom, the knowledge of what is good and bad. One of the positions suggested by Socrates as an option, namely that the virtues, like different parts of a piece of gold, are entirely similar, though not identical, seems vacuous: it is introduced simply to get a clear view of the contrasted possibilities. If this is so, there are only two, not three, main options: the identity view and the view, espoused by Protagoras, that the virtues are distinct and independent. But, even on the identity view, there remains a problem, as we can see from Stoic discussions of the question: What are we to make of the fact that there are five (or perhaps more) different names of this allegedy single condition, virtue? They do not seem to be related merely arbitrarily, like two names of a single city (e.g., "Istanbul" and "Constantinople"), but seem in at least some cases rather to apply to virtue through its relation to the different types of acts—just acts, pious acts, courageous acts, and so forth—in which virtue is exercised in different circumstances. We still want to know how to characterize these different manifestations of virtue and their relations to each other. Even on the identity view suggested by Socrates, then, the question of the unity of virtue remains highly complicated.

(VI) The Relations Between Particular Virtues

Let us now briefly consider some of the issues raised by the four particular arguments that make up this central argument about the unity of virtue.

The first argument (330b6–332a3) concerns the unity of justice and piety. One remarkable thing about this argument is that it explicitly assumes that justice is just (330c4–8) and that piety is pious, indeed that if anything is pious, piety is (330d8 ff.). What is even more remarkable is that both Protagoras and Socrates seem to accept this curious claim without comment, as if it were an obvious, basic truth. This is perhaps the earliest occurrence in Plato of what scholars have come to call "self-predication." Plato freely uses statements in which the predicate "F" is ascribed to an item, F-ness, as if such statements as "heat is hot," "difference is different," "oddness is odd," were trivially true. This is extremely puzzling. To us, most of these statements seem absurdly false. As a rule, a feature is not an instance of itself, and to assume so amounts to a "category mistake." Color itself does not seem to be the kind of item which we could say is colored. Nevertheless, such statements play a prominent role in Plato's later metaphysics. There is considerable scholarly debate about how Plato might have dealt with the difficulties they raise. This is not the place to review this debate, let alone to take a stand in it, but to understand the argument of the *Protagoras* the following may be of some help.

(i) Suppose Socrates is just. In that case, we might ask what it is about him that is just. We might answer by specifying some feature which is precisely what is just about Socrates. So there would be something, namely in fact his justice, of which we are willing to say that this is what is just about Socrates. Further, we might think that it was precisely this feature which was what was just about any just person. So, in this sense, we might be prepared to say that it is this feature, justice, which is just. In saying this we would, of course, be quite aware that justice is not just in the same way and sense in which Socrates is just. Socrates is just, it would seem, by *having* this feature, justice. Justice rather would be just by *being* this feature.

(ii) Suppose we say that water is wet, and that whatever else is wet is wet because it has some water mixed into it. One might then identify water with wetness and think that it was a trivial, but basic, truth that wetness (i.e., water) is wet; and that, if wetness were not wet, nothing else would be wet, because whatever else is wet is wet because it has a share of (partakes of, is appropriately related to) water. This, again, would not mean that water is wet in the same way or sense in which a piece of cloth is wet. The latter is wet by somehow *having* some wetness, the former by *being* wetness or water.

(iii) We need to keep in mind that in Plato's day abstract nouns were still rare; in fact, Plato himself contributed significantly to the formation of abstract names to correspond to adjectives, and in the *Theaetetus* he apologizes for coining the general abstract noun, "quality" (182a). Instead of abstract nouns, one used the neuter adjective with the definite article: "the hot" instead of "heat," "the ill" instead of "illness," "the beautiful" instead of "beauty." Now, if one used "the wet" and "wetness" interchangeably, it would be natural to think that in some sense wetness is wet, for it seems obvious that there is a sense in which the wet is wet.

Moreover, only the use of abstract nouns makes it seem at all natural to assume that there even are corresponding general abstract features. It is, of course, difficult to see in what sense an abstract feature could be self-predicational, how wetness could be wet, for example. But if, instead of wetness, coldness, and so on, we think of the wet, the cold, the hot, the ill, it is by no means obvious that we should think of these as abstract features. We might rather think of them on the model of stuffs; for example, of the wet on the model of water, or some wet-making stuff, rather than as an abstract feature, though we might well be aware that this can be no more than a model or an analogy. In fact, some philosophers before Plato (for example, Anaxagoras, but also some doctors) clearly think of qualities as stuffs, as ingredients in a mixture which constitutes an object. Even much later, the Stoics, and doctors influenced by them, think of qualities in this way. Against this background, then, we should not be surprised if Plato has no difficulty in making such claims as "justice is just," as if they were trivial truths, even though he does have considerable difficulty in spelling out the precise force of this, once he gets interested in clarifying the metaphysical status of such items as justice. Here in the *Protagoras* he seems to content himself with the assumption that there really is such a thing as justice (330c1), and that it is just, if anything is.

Suppose, then, we understand "justice is just" as the claim that what is just about somebody—what, for instance, reliably produces just actions when they are called for—is a person's justice. How does this help to understand Socrates' argument? If we assume that piety is merely a form of justice, namely justice in one's dealings with the gods, there would be a ready sense in which, as Socrates also asserts, justice is pious and piety is just. What it would be about Socrates which is pious, which would reliably produce pious actions, would be his justice; and what could be relied upon to produce just actions, at least in his dealings with the gods, would be piety. In this case, justice and piety would not be, as Protagoras supposes, quite unlike each other, separate and independent. Whether or not they are identical, Socrates would have shown all he needs to refute Protagoras.

Next follows an argument that wisdom and temperance are the same (332a3–333b6), and the beginning of an argument that justice and temperance go together (333b ff.), which, however, Protagoras does not allow to arrive at a formal conclusion (cf. 334a3 ff.). In the case of justice and temperance, it is clear enough that they are related, and that these are not two entirely independent, separate abilities, united only by the fact that both are required by a certain conception of what it is to be virtuous or good. Obviously justice requires a certain amount of temperance, in the sense of self-restraint; that one recognize and respect the boundary between oneself and others; that one not let oneself be carried away beyond one's limits to invade or violate somebody else. Actually, "temperance" and "self-restraint" are somewhat one-sided translations of the Greek term *sōphrosunē*, which might more literally be rendered "soundness of mind." It is soundness of mind that lets one see one's limits and not transgress them, and so be self-restrained or temperate. If we choose this rendering, it also becomes more obvious that the subjects of the previous argument, wisdom and temperance (or soundness of mind), cannot be entirely separate and unrelated: clearly, to be wise must minimally require soundness of mind. As in the case of justice and piety, the different virtues are intricately related in a way that needs sorting out if we want to know precisely what would make us good or virtuous.

After the major interruption provoked by Protagoras at 334c7, the overall argument resumes only at 348c5. There Socrates recalls the original questions and the stand Protagoras had taken, but allows him, in the light of the previous argument, to shift his position and to claim now that the virtues are the different parts of virtue, but that four of them, namely wisdom, justice, piety, and self-restraint, are quite alike, whereas courage is quite different from them (349d2–8). At 351b3, Socrates begins a complex argument against this view, in favor of the conclusion that courage, too, is a matter of wisdom or knowledge.

This argument is full of puzzling and interesting detail. Perhaps the greatest difficulty for the interpreter is that Socrates seems to rely on the assumption that the good is what is pleasant (cf. 351e5–6), or even that "good" and "pleasant" are interchangeable (355b3 ff.). This suggests some form of hedonism, i.e., a view to the effect that pleasure is the highest good, that pleasure is what we in fact do, or should, aim at in our lives. It is a position some version of which, at least, Plato vehemently rejects in the *Gorgias* (495a ff.), in the *Republic* (505b ff.), and in the *Philebus* (20e ff.). It is difficult to determine precisely what position it is, among the great number of possibilities, that Socrates means to be arguing from here. It is clear that he assumes, against Protagoras' objection, that the pleasant as such is good (cf. 351c1 ff.). If pleasures are objectionable, it is not because they are bad in themselves, but because of their bad consequences. He also clearly assumes that a good life is a pleasant life (cf.351b4 ff.), perhaps even the most pleasant life. But this, of course, is perfectly compatible with the view (adopted by Plato even in the *Philebus* and, with qualification, by Aristotle) that, though the good we aim at is not pleasure, but something else, nevertheless the good life turns out to be the most pleasant life, and, what is more, that pleasure contributes directly and in its own right to the goodness of life.

But, further on in the argument, Socrates seems to assume not only that the pleasant as such is good, but that it is with reference to their pleasantness and nothing else that things are called "good" (cf., e.g., 354b5 ff.; d1 ff.; d7 ff.; 355a3 ff.). This does sound as if now the pleasant is treated not only as a good, but as the supreme good we aim at in all our actions: a position incompatible with what Plato makes Socrates say in other dialogues. Now, in considering this, we need to keep in mind the following:

(i) Socrates uses the hedonist thesis in the context of his rebuttal to an objection raised by the common man, to whom Socrates also attributes the hedonist thesis itself. For his argument that even courage is nothing but wisdom, Socrates wants to claim that knowledge or wisdom cannot be overcome by any motive, in particular not by fear. This runs into the objection that it is commonly believed that, overcome by passion, we often act against our better judgment. But the upshot of this part of the argument is that, given the hedonist thesis, it does not make sense to say, as the common man does, that one acts against one's better judgment in such cases. Since the common man also accepts the hedonist thesis, he is refuted: either he is wrong in his assumption that knowledge can be overcome by passion or he is in no position to make this claim, since it contradicts his hedonism. In this way Socrates neutralizes his objection, but we need not think of Socrates himself as committed to the hedonist thesis.

(ii) Given the appropriate assumptions about the mind (more about these below), the arguments in this section can be reformulated without relying on a hedonist thesis.

(iii) The text goes out of its way to indicate that the term "pleasant" admits of a variety of interpretations. "Pleasant" may not just mean "pleasurable," in the sense of "providing one with pleasure." It also may cover anything which is not painful (cf. 355a3; 358b4). More important, it might refer to things which satisfy in other ways than by giving pleasure, a point dwelt on at some length in 358a5 ff. Indeed, at 358a, Socrates explicitly says that when, in this context, he speaks of what is pleasant, he is ignoring certain distinctions between kinds of pleasure, satisfaction, enjoyment, elation, and so forth. So perhaps it is perfectly acceptable for Socrates to say that we aim at the pleasant, that the pleasant is not just good but *the* good. He might mean by this that we aim at what satisfies our needs.

Whatever may be the position Socrates attributes to the common man, it is worth commenting briefly on the fact that, and the question why, Socrates denies that there is such a thing as *akrasia* or weakness of will—that we sometimes are, as the common man supposes, driven by passion to act against our better judgment. Indeed, the very term *akrasia*, which we then find in Aristotle and later, may come from this passage (cf. 352c5; d2), as does the image of reason as the slave of the passions (cf. 352b4; b7–8; c1). Plato and Aristotle, each in his own way, will disagree with Socrates on this point, whereas the Stoics will revert to Socrates' position.

Now, one might think that, for his denial of *akrasia*, Socrates relies on some claim about the special power of knowledge or wisdom. Perhaps, one might think, he holds that if one really knows what is right, no amount of passion of whatever kind can cause one to act contrary to one's knowledge; that failure to act rightly just reveals that one does not really fully know what is right. But it becomes apparent later (cf. 358b7; c7; d1) that the Socratic claim is the much stronger one that nobody acts even against his beliefs, much less his knowledge. That is to say, the claim does not rely on some special power attributed to knowledge as distinct from mere opinion. Hence Socrates must assume that somebody who, on the face of it, believes that he should do X because it is good, but nevertheless fails to do it, does not really believe that to do X is good, but believes that, on balance, to do X is bad. The passage at 358d5 ff. provides a clue to how Socrates can think this. There he characterizes fear as a certain kind of belief, namely, as the expectation of something bad. Hence, he seems to assume, if one fails to do X out of fear, despite believing that it would be good to do it, this really means that one believes that the bad expected from doing X outweighs the expected good; and that therefore, on balance, it is not good after all to do X, but bad. If the other passions (e.g., desire, pleasure, pain) are also characterized as beliefs about what is good or bad, then Socrates can describe what the common man takes to be conflicts between reason and passion, in which one's considered judgment is sometimes overwhelmed, as mere conflicts of belief, to be settled by a rational calculation of expected consequences. He can then deny that anyone ever acts against his belief about what, on balance, it is good for him to do.

If we find this highly intellectualistic account of the passions as judgments of some kind implausible, we should keep in mind that it is only Plato, in the *Republic* (IV, 437b ff.), who, precisely to explain how one can act against the judgment of one's reason, for the first time introduces different parts of the soul, each with its own desires, allowing us to understand how irrational desire may overcome the dictates of desire and reason. Here in the *Protagoras*, Socrates seems to argue as if the soul just were reason, and the passions were reasoned beliefs or judgments of some kind, and as if, therefore, we were entirely guided or motivated by beliefs of one kind or another. On this picture of the soul, it is easy to see why Socrates thinks that nobody acts against his knowledge or even his beliefs: nothing apart from beliefs could motivate such an action.

Although no assumption about the special power of knowledge, as opposed to mere belief or opinion, is needed for his denial of *akrasia*, Socrates does want to claim that knowledge or wisdom provides one with a special ability or strength that mere belief does not. This is what Socrates turns to next (356c4 ff.).

The point is this. In some respects, in certain areas, phenomena are systematically misleading; hence the beliefs based on them are systematically misguided. If we did not have some independent body of knowledge, on the basis of which we knew better, and if we just followed appearances, we would end up with the wrong beliefs. Plato is particularly impressed with one kind of case, which he first refers to here, but also discusses in greater detail in the *Sophist* (235e ff.): optical illusions caused by viewing objects from nearby and from afar. For example, tall columns, seen from the ground directly below, would look impossibly thin at the top if they were really straight; they have to be thicker at the upper end so as to look reasonably straight. A mathematical formula determines the correct proportions. Ultimately, only applying the correct optical theory can protect us against being misled by such appearances. What is true for apparent size is also true for pleasure and pain, as Plato will point out again in the *Philebus* (41e ff.), drawing on the same analogy. Nearby pleasures and pains seem large, while those far in the future seem smaller. Accordingly, falling prey to a kind of illusion, we systematically tend to overestimate present pains and pleasures, and underestimate pleasures and pains in the more distant future. But this means that our beliefs concerning them, which guide our actions, are systematically distorted unless we have a theory, a calculus of pleasure and pain, to correct them. Hence knowledge, some kind of science, seems to be needed if we are to avoid making the wrong choices and thus ruining our lives (cf. 356e2; e6; e8; 357a6–7).

Obviously, this part of the argument still rests on the hedonistic assumption that we aim at pleasure (and nothing else); but it need not do so. What is true of pleasure and pain, namely, that they are systematically misestimated depending on the distance, is generally true of whatever is held good or bad. If we are guided by the systematically distorted beliefs about good and bad that naturally arise from appearances and gain acceptance in our communities, thus reinforcing our own illusions, we shall ruin our lives. Only knowledge, a calculus of goods to correct our misleading beliefs, can save us. This is one reason why knowledge, as opposed to mere true belief, is so crucial. Mere belief, even if true, always is threatened by the powerful but illusory evidence of appearance.

Socrates has thus suggested a conception of knowledge or wisdom on which it not only cannot be overwhelmed by the passions, but is decisive for our lives, because it determines how we act, so that we live a maximally good and satisfying life. Now, at 359a2, he can finally return to the relation between wisdom and courage. Are they, as Protagoras had insisted, quite unlike each other, so that one may well be courageous but not wise, or wise but not courageous? Given the notion of wisdom Socrates has developed, it is obvious that courage is just wisdom, and that fear will not prevent the wise person from doing what is courageous. Being wise, one will know what is bad. One will not be oblivious to the dangers of a situation. Otherwise one would just be rash or stupid. But one will also know that what appears so frightful, and thus is shunned by cowards, in fact, on balance, is not. What appears frightful, in the light of one's corrective knowledge, will be seen at worst to be less awful than what would result from the opposite course of action. One will know that the really terrible thing, the thing really to be afraid of, would be to fail to do what the situation demands. Thus cowardice turns out to be ignorance, a failure to calculate properly what is to be feared and what is not.

(VII) Conclusion

In this way, then, the long argument concerning the unity of the virtues comes to a conclusion. Being virtuous, Socrates suggests, is being wise, possessing a science or an art of properly evaluating things. It would seem that Protagoras was right to claim that virtue can be taught, that it is an art, a matter of wisdom. Where Protagoras went wrong was in abandoning this insight. By following common belief and separating the virtues from each other, and in particular by insisting that courage is altogether different from wisdom, Protagoras showed that he had not thought things out to their conclusion, and that he was confused concerning virtue, the very subject on which he claimed expertise.

But Socrates, in his concluding remarks (361c2 ff.), tellingly does not assume that we have now seen what virtue is and that it can be taught. All we have been shown is that Protagoras is confused, that he does not know what virtue is and whether it can be taught, and hence that he can hardly be qualified to teach virtue. It is true, we also have seen a way of looking at the matter on which virtue would be wisdom and so could be taught (in the sense in which wisdom can be taught—a further question Protagoras' great speech will have already suggested, but which now presses itself on us without being raised explicitly). But whether this is the right way to look at things, Socrates himself insists, only further and more thorough *skepsis*, further inquiry, can show (cf. 361c6; 361d6).

Hence Socrates would like to continue the discussion with Protagoras, but Protagoras has had enough for now. So Socrates leaves, only to run into a friend, the friend he meets at the beginning of the dialogue, and to whom he then tells the whole story of his encounter first with Hippocrates and then with the great sophist himself. This allows him, if not to continue the discussion with Protagoras, at least to go over the argument with him again by recounting it. It is an argument worth going over again and again; but not because, by going over it, we might finally uncover the veiled truth, the wisdom, it is ready to reveal to the reader who is willing to listen diligently and to follow its clues for long enough. Already in antiquity, many believed that the dialogues of Plato contained a hidden truth, or at least hinted at the true doctrine. But the power of the *Protagoras* seems to be precisely that, instead of closing off and seeming to settle questions, it always provides us with new questions to pursue, new ways to look at familiar things, which, though certainly illuminating, in turn can be and often are questioned themselves. Surely, if wisdom can be taught, it is not by being told the truth—such a truth one would not know how to make one's own—but by being moved to look at things oneself, to consider and reconsider them in all their complexity, from all angles, until, if ever, one arrives at a view of one's own that seems to remain stable however much one is prepared to reconsider it. In this sense, though written with great art to embed it firmly in its time and place, the *Protagoras* continues to provoke us to pursue basic questions about our lives, and the way we think about them, with an amazing freshness and directness.

Keble College, Oxford
November 1991

SELECTED BIBLIOGRAPHY

BACKGROUND:

Adkins, A. W. H. *Merit and Responsibility*. Oxford: Oxford University Press, 1960.

Arieti, J. A. *Interpreting Plato: The Dialogues as Drama*. Lanham, MD: Rowman and Littlefield, 1991.

Gosling, J., and C. Taylor. *The Greeks on Pleasure*. Oxford: Oxford University Press, 1982.

Guthrie, W. K. C. *A History of Greek Philosophy*, vols. III, IV. Cambridge: Cambridge University Press, 1969, 1975.

Irwin, T. *Plato's Moral Theory*. Oxford: Oxford University Press, 1977.

Kerferd, G. B. *The Sophistic Movement*. Cambridge: Cambridge University Press, 1981.

O'Brien, M. J. *The Socratic Paradoxes and the Greek Mind*. Chapel Hill: University of North Carolina Press, 1967.

Nussbaum, M. *The Fragility of Goodness*. Cambridge: Cambridge University Press, 1986.

Roberts, J. W. *City of Socrates: An Introduction to Classical Athens*. London: Routledge and Kegan Paul, 1984.

Robinson, R. *Plato's Earlier Dialectic*, 2d ed. Oxford: Oxford University Press, 1953.
Taylor, A. E. *Plato, The Man and His Work*. London: Methuen, 1926.
Vlastos, G. *Socrates, Ironist and Moral Philosopher*. Ithaca: Cornell University Press, 1991.

COMMENTARIES:

Hubbard, B., and E. Carnofsky. *Plato's Protagoras: A Socratic Commentary*. London: Duckworth, 1982.
Taylor, C. C. W. *Plato, Protagoras*. Oxford: Oxford University Press, 1976.

ARTICLES:

Adkins, A. W. H. "Arete, Techne, Democracy and Sophists: *Protagoras* 316b–328d." *Journal of Hellenic Studies* 93 (1973): 3.
Duncan, R. "Courage in Plato's *Protagoras*." *Phronesis* 23 (1978): 216.
Gagarin, M. "The Purpose of Plato's *Protagoras*." *Transactions of the American Philological Society* 100 (1969): 133.
Gallop, D. "Justice and Holiness in *Protagoras* 330–331." *Phronesis* 6 (1961): 86.
_____. "The Socratic Paradox in the *Protagoras*." *Phronesis* 9 (1964): 117.
Grube, G. M. A. "The Structural Unity of the *Protagoras*." *Classical Quarterly* 27 (1933): 203.
Gulley, N. "Socrates' Thesis at *Protagoras* 358b–c." *Phoenix* 25 (1971): 118.
Hackforth, R. "Hedonism in Plato's *Protagoras*." *Classical Quarterly* 22 (1928): 39.
Kahn, C. "Plato on the Unity of the Virtues." In *Facets of Plato's Philosophy*, edited by W. H. Werkmeister. Assen: Van Gorcum, 1976.
Kerferd, G. B. "Protagoras' Doctrine of Justice and Virtue in the *Protagoras*." *Journal of Hellenic Studies* 73 (1953): 42.
Penner, T. "The Unity of Virtue." *Philosophical Review* 82 (1973): 35.
Rosenmeyer, T. "Plato and Mass Words." *Transactions of the American Philological Society* 88 (1957): 88.
Santas, G. "Plato's *Protagoras* and Explanations of Weakness." *Philosophical Review* 75 (1966): 3.
Sesonske, A. "Hedonism in the *Protagoras*." *Journal of the History of Philosophy* 1 (1963): 73.
Sullivan, J.P. "The Hedonism in Plato's *Protagoras*." *Phronesis* 6 (1961): 10.
Vlastos, G. "Socrates on Acrasia." *Phoenix* 23 (1969): 71.
_____. "The Unity of the Virtues in the *Protagoras*." *The Review of Metaphysics* 25 (1972): 415.
Weiss, R. "Hedonism in the *Protagoras* and the Sophist's Guarantee." *Ancient Philosophy* (1990): 17.

TRANSLATORS' PREFACE

Plato is preeminent not only as a philosopher but also as a dramatic artist in Greek prose. We have tried to fashion a translation of *Protagoras* that gives good account of the dialogue both as a philosophical text and as a literary masterpiece. As literature, Plato's dialogues demand of the translator sensitivity to a wide range of styles. In *Protagoras*, to take the case at hand, each sophist has his own rhetorical style. And Plato allows Socrates to parody the style of Protagoras as well as that of Hippias, another of the sophists present. Socrates' own speaking style (which does double duty as the narrative framework in this dialogue) has a naturalness and elegance that cannot be reproduced in English simply by replicating the sentence structure of the Greek. The temptation to do so is great, for English is flexible and capacious enough to mimic Greek fairly closely and still be comprehensible and even stylistically acceptable. But tone is everything in literary art. The lexical meanings of words have to be balanced with word order, sentence rhythms, the sheer sounds of syllables, nuances of usage, and other similar considerations. Plato paid a great deal of attention to these things in composing Greek such as might be heard in the Athens of his day, and so should his translators in composing analogous contemporary American English.

At the same time Plato's translators must assume that in his texts everything is of potential philosophical significance. Nothing may be added, deleted, or altered that might possibly affect that significance. But every act of translation is an interpretation that entails certain consequences. Take a key word in *Protagoras*, *aretē*. Should this be translated as "virtue" (the traditional translation) or as "excellence" (lexically close to the Greek meaning and used more and more by translators)?

The problem with "virtue" as a translation is that the word has, in its centuries of evolution from the Latin *virtus* (literally, "manliness"), acquired certain moral and theological connotations that *aretē* never had in Greek. At the same time it has lost most of its significance as a term of social approbation. Every Greek wanted to be known for his *aretē*, his superior intellectual, physical, and moral qualities. "Virtuous," when it is not an arch synonym for "chaste," is now used mostly of people who have some mild degree of self-discipline or industry (as in abstaining from chocolates or in exercising regularly) and is almost always tinged with irony ("My, aren't we being virtuous today?"). The noun "virtue" is scarcely used at all in everyday speech any more except in the general sense of an advantage or strength ("This program has the virtue of allowing multiple entry points") or in phrases such as "by virtue of . . ." (both of these usages in fact preserve an old meaning of the word— "potent quality"—that is very close to what *aretē* meant). "Virtue," a word that from the early Renaissance (cf. the Italian *virtù*) has epitomized in Europe and America a mainstream tradition of political and ethical values, has lost much of its virtue.

"Excellence," on the other hand, is now coming into vogue as a term connoting the high standards of performance and achievement valued by our society. Americans, as individuals and as a society, want to be the best—excellent at everything they do—or at least aim at lofty goals, and this is certainly a kind of *aretē*. But we do not speak of courage, moderation, or wisdom as "excellences." "Excellence" may be emerging as a state of mind, but it does not have the complex particularity or the weight of tradition that "virtue" does have and that *aretē* had in Greek culture. If that tradition has been partly forgotten, it would not be inappropriate for a new translation of Plato to reintroduce it into the consciousness of its readers. We have chosen to translate *aretē* as "virtue," with the intent of reinvigorating contemporary language and usage rather than simply reflecting it.

Similar considerations are involved in the translation of other important terms in the dialogue. In general we have aimed at consistency, that is, rendering a given Greek word by the same English word whenever it occurs. This is not always possible (see notes at 320d and 345d). A word such as *sōphrosunē* (soundness of mind, self-control, temperance, prudence, sense of decency) covers more lexical territory than any one English word can map (see the note at 329c). Moreover, Plato, as much as he was fond of definitions and distinctions, was not the sort of philosopher who develops a consistent technical terminology and builds a philosophical system upon it.

We have used Burnet's Oxford Classical Text as the basis for this translation.

Stanley Lombardo, Classics, University of Kansas
Karen Bell, Philosophy, California State University, Fresno

January 1992

PROTAGORAS

FRIEND: Where have you just come from, Socrates?[1] No, don't tell me. It's pretty obvious that you've been hunting the ripe and ready Alcibiades.[2] Well, I saw him just the other day, and he is certainly still a beautiful man—and just between the two of us, 'man' is the proper word, Socrates: his beard is already filling out.

SOCRATES: Well, what of it? I thought you were an admirer of Homer,[3] who says that youth is most charming when the beard is first blooming—which is just the stage Alcibiades is at.

FRIEND: So what's up? Were you just with him? And how is the young man disposed towards you?

SOCRATES: Pretty well, I think, especially today, since he rallied to my side and said a great many things to support me.[4] You're right, of course: I *was* just with him. But there's something really strange I want to tell you about. Although we were together, I

b

---

1. Socrates (469–399 B.C.), an Athenian whose mature life was devoted to discussing ethical questions with any and all interested persons, in a characteristic way which has come to be considered as one of the central methods of philosophizing in western culture. Plato was greatly influenced by Socrates, and he used Socrates as a speaker in nearly all of his dialogues. Socrates was put to death on charges of impiety and corrupting the young. The dramatic date of the dialogue is probably in the late 430's; Socrates is in his late 30's, Alcibiades in his late teens, and Protagoras in his late 50's.

2. Alcibiades (c. 450–404 B.C.), Athenian, son of Cleinias, noted in his youth for his great beauty and intellectual promise; later notorious for his alleged acts of religious desecration and denounced for betrayal of his city when he fought for Sparta in the later stages of the Peloponnesian War. Alcibiades is a major participant in Plato's *Symposium*, and it is from his encomium of Socrates in that dialogue that we learn much about Socrates' personal character and the relationship between the two of them, at least as Plato understood it.

3. Homer, *Iliad*, 24.348; *Odyssey*, 10.279. Homer (epic poet active in the eighth century B.C.) has been rightly called the educator of all Greece. He is cited frequently by Plato (five times in this dialogue).

4. The reference here is to the events described at 336b and 347b, in which Alcibiades intervenes in the discussions so as to smooth the way for Socrates to proceed as Socrates prefers.

didn't pay him any mind; in fact, I forgot all about him most of the time.

c   FRIEND: How could anything like that have happened to the two of you? You surely haven't met someone else more beautiful, at least not in this city.

SOCRATES: Much more beautiful.

FRIEND: What are you saying? A citizen or a foreigner?

SOCRATES: A foreigner.

FRIEND: From where?

SOCRATES: Abdera.

FRIEND: And this foreigner seems to you more beautiful than the son of Cleinias?

SOCRATES: How could superlative wisdom not seem surpassingly beautiful?

FRIEND: What! Have you been in the company of some wise man, Socrates?

d   SOCRATES: The wisest man alive, if you think the wisest man is—Protagoras.[5]

FRIEND: What are you saying? Is Protagoras in town?

SOCRATES: And has been for two days.

FRIEND: And you've just now come from being with him?

310   SOCRATES: That's right, and took part in quite a long conversation.

FRIEND: Well, sit right down, if you're free now, and tell us all about it. Let the boy make room for you here.

SOCRATES: By all means. I'd count it a favor if you'd listen.

FRIEND: And vice versa, if you'd tell us.

SOCRATES: That would make it a double favor then. Well, here's the story.

b   This morning just before daybreak, while it was still dark, Hippocrates,[6] son of Apollodoros and Phason's brother, banged on my door with his stick, and when it was opened for him he

5. Protagoras of Abdera (in Thrace), one of the earliest and most successful sophists. His dates are uncertain; he probably died around 415 B.C. at the age of 70. When the Athenians founded Thurii in 444, Protagoras was invited to draw up the new colony's constitution. The extant fragments of Protagoras are found in Diels-Krantz 80 (translation by Kathleen Freeman, *Ancilla to the Pre-Socratic Philosophers*). Protagoras' most famous dictum (which is not referred to in this dialogue) is "Of all things Man is the measure, both of things that are, that they are, and of things that are not, that they are not."

6. This Hippocrates was probably a historical person, but no other information about him survives.

barged right in and yelled in that voice of his, "Socrates, are you awake or asleep?"

Recognizing his voice, I said, "Is that Hippocrates? No bad news, I hope."

"Nothing but good news," he said.

"I'd like to hear it," I said. "What brings you here at such an hour?"

"Protagoras has arrived," he said, standing next to me.

"Day before yesterday," I said. "Did you just find out?"

"Yes! Just last evening." As he said this he felt around for the   c
bed and sat at my feet and continued: "That's right, late yesterday evening, after I got back from Oenoë. My slave Satyros had run away from me. I meant to tell you that I was going after him, but something else came up and made me forget. After I got back and we had eaten dinner and were about to get some rest, *then* my brother tells me Protagoras has arrived. I was getting ready to come right over to see you even then, until I realized it was just too late at night. But as soon as I had slept   d
some and wasn't dead-tired any more, I got up and came over here right away."

Recognizing his fighting spirit and his excitement, I asked him: "So what's it to you? Has Protagoras done anything wrong to you?"

He laughed and said, "You bet he has, Socrates. He has a monopoly on wisdom and won't give me any."

"But look," I said, "if you meet his price he'll make you wise too."

"If only it were as simple as that," he said, "I'd bankrupt   e
myself and my friends too. But that's why I'm coming to you, so you will talk to him for me. I'm too young myself, and besides, I've never even seen Protagoras or heard him speak. I was still just a child the last time he was in town. He's such a celebrity, Socrates, and everyone says he's a terribly clever speaker. Why   311
don't we walk over now, to be sure to catch him in? I've heard he's staying with Callias, son of Hipponicus. Come on, let's go."

"Let's not go there just yet," I said. "It's too early. Why don't we go out here into the courtyard and stroll around until it's light? Then we can go. Protagoras spends most of his time indoors, so don't worry; we're likely to catch him in."

So we got up and walked around the courtyard. I wanted to see what Hippocrates was made of, so I started to examine him   b
with a few questions. "Tell me, Hippocrates," I said. "You're

trying to get access to Protagoras, prepared to pay him a cash fee for his services to you. But what is he, and what do you expect to become? I mean, suppose you had your mind set on going to your namesake, Hippocrates of Cos,[7] the famous physi-

c   cian, to pay him a fee for his services to you, and if someone asked you what this Hippocrates is that you were going to pay him, what would you say?"

"I would say a physician," he said.

"And what would you expect to become?"

"A physician."

"And if you had a mind to go to Polycleitus of Argos or Pheidias[8] of Athens to pay them a fee, and if somebody were to ask you what kind of professionals you had in mind paying, what would you say?"

"I would say sculptors."

"And what would you expect to become?"

"A sculptor, obviously."

d   "All right," I said. "Here we are, you and I, on our way to Protagoras, prepared to pay him cash as a fee on your behalf, spending our own money, and if that's not enough to persuade him, our friends' money as well. Suppose someone notices our enthusiasm and asks us: 'Tell me, Socrates and Hippocrates,

e   what is your idea in paying Protagoras? What is he?' What would we say to him? What other name do we hear in reference to Protagoras? Pheidias is called a sculptor and Homer a poet. What do we hear Protagoras called?"

"A sophist is what they call him, anyway, Socrates."

"Then it is as a sophist that we are going to pay him?"

"Yes."

312   "And if somebody asks you what you expect to become in going to Protagoras?"

He blushed in response—there was just enough daylight now to show him up—and said, "If this is at all like the previous cases, then, obviously, to become a sophist."

---

7. Hippocrates of Cos (469–399 B.C.), an exact contemporary of Socrates, was renowned in his time and to posterity as a powerful physician and healer. He was perhaps the first to theorize both about the causes of disease and the unique ethical responsibilities of the physician.

8. Polycleitus, a sculptor who flourished during the last half of the fifth century B.C., was renowned for his statue of Hera at Argos. Pheidias (an exact contemporary of Plato) was also a sculptor; he was renowned for the statue of Athena in the Parthenon and the Zeus at Olympia.

"What? You? Wouldn't you be ashamed to present yourself to the Greek world as a sophist?"

"Yes, I would, Socrates, to be perfectly honest."

"Well, look, Hippocrates, maybe this isn't the sort of education you expect to get from Protagoras. Maybe you expect to get the kind of lessons you got from your grammar instructor or   b
music teacher or wrestling coach. You didn't get from them technical instruction to become a professional, but a general education suitable for a gentleman."

"That's it exactly! That's just the sort of education you get from Protagoras."

"Then do you know what you are about to do now, or does it escape you?" I said.

"What do you mean?"

"That you are about to hand over your soul for treatment to a   c
man who is, as you say, a sophist. As to what exactly a sophist is, I would be surprised if you really knew. And yet, if you are ignorant of this, you don't know whether you are entrusting your soul to something good or bad."

"But I think I do know," he said.

"Then tell me what you think a sophist is."

"I think," he said, "that, as the name suggests, he is someone who has an understanding of wise things."[9]

"Well, you could say the same thing about painters and carpenters, that they understand wise things. But if someone asked   d
us 'wise in what respect?' we would probably answer, for painters, 'wise as far as making images is concerned,' and so on for the other cases. And if someone asked, 'What about sophists? What wise things do they understand?'—what would we answer? What are they expert at making?"

"What else, Socrates, should we say a sophist is expert at than making people clever speakers?"

"Our answer would then be true, but not sufficient, for it requires another question: On what subject does the sophist make you a clever speaker? For example, a lyre-player makes   e
you a clever speaker on his subject of expertise, the lyre. Right?"

"Yes."

<hr />

9. Hippocrates is mistakenly deriving the Greek word for sophist, *sophistēs*, from the base *soph-* (wise) and the base *ist-* (know). In fact the *ist-* in this word is simply part of an agent-forming suffix.

"All right then. On what subject does a sophist make you a clever speaker?"

"It's clear that it's the same subject that he understands."

"Likely enough. And what is this subject that the sophist understands and makes his student understand?"

"By God," he said, "I really don't know what to say."

313　　I went on to my next point: "Do you see what kind of danger you are about to put your soul in? If you had to entrust your body to someone and risk its becoming healthy or ill, you would consider carefully whether you should entrust it or not, and you would confer with your family and friends for days on end. But when it comes to something you value more than your body,

b　　namely your soul, and when everything concerning whether you do well or ill in your life depends on whether it becomes worthy or worthless, I don't see you getting together with your father or brother or a single one of your friends to consider whether or not to entrust your soul to this recently arrived stranger. No, you hear about him in the evening—right?—and the next morning, here you are, not to talk about whether it's a good idea to entrust yourself to him or not, but ready to spend your own money and your friends' as well, as if you had thought it all through already and, no matter what, you had to

c　　be with Protagoras, a man whom you admit you don't know and have never conversed with, and whom you call a sophist although you obviously have no idea what this sophist is to whom you are about to entrust yourself."

"I guess so, Socrates, from what you say."

"Am I right, then, Hippocrates, that a sophist is a kind of merchant[10] who peddles provisions upon which the soul is nourished? That's what he seems like to me."

"But what is the soul nourished on, Socrates?"

d　　"Teachings, I would say. And watch, or the sophist might deceive us in advertising what he sells, the way merchants who market food for the body do. In general, those who market provisions don't know what is good or bad for the body—they just recommend everything they sell—nor do those who buy (unless one happens to be a trainer or doctor). In the same way, those who take their teachings from town to town and sell them

---

10. In his later dialogue *Sophist*, Plato again uses the image of the merchant, characterizing the sophist as a seller of "merchandise of the soul which is concerned with speech and the knowledge of virtue" (224d).

wholesale or retail to anybody who wants them recommend all
their products, but I wouldn't be surprised, my friend, if some of
these people did not know which of their products are beneficial and which detrimental to the soul. Likewise those who buy   e
from them, unless one happens to be a physician of the soul. So
if you are a knowledgeable consumer, you can buy teachings
safely from Protagoras or anyone else. But if you're not, please
don't risk what is most dear to you on a roll of the dice, for there   314
is a far greater risk in buying teachings than in buying food.
When you buy food and drink from the merchant you can take
each item back home from the store in its own container and
before you ingest it into your body you can lay it all out and call
in an expert for consultation as to what should be eaten or
drunk and what not, and how much and when. So there's not   b
much risk in your purchase. But you cannot carry teachings
away in a separate container. You put down your money and
take the teaching away in your soul by having learned it, and off
you go, either helped or injured. Anyway, these are the questions we should look into, with the help of our elders. You and I
are still a little too young to get to the bottom of such a great
matter. Well, let's do what we had started out to do and go hear
this man; and after we have heard him, we can talk with some
others also. Protagoras isn't the only one there. There's Hippias   c
of Elis too, and also Prodicus of Ceos, I believe. And many
others as well, wise men all."

Having agreed on this, we set out. When we got to the doorway we stood there discussing some point which had come up
along the road and which we didn't want to leave unsettled
before we went in. So we were standing there in the doorway
discussing it until we reached an agreement, and I think the
doorman, a eunuch, overheard us. He must have been annoyed   d
with all the traffic of sophists in and out of the house, because
when we knocked he opened the door, took one look at us and
said, ''Ha! More sophists! He's busy.'' Then he slammed the
door in our faces with both hands as hard as he could. We
knocked again, and he answered through the locked door,
''Didn't you hear me say he's busy?'' ''My good man,'' I said,
''we haven't come to see Callias,[11] and we are not sophists.''   e

---

11. Callias (c. 450–370 B.C.), a wealthy Athenian and patron of culture, often
ridiculed for his extravagance.

Calm down. We want to see Protagoras. That's why we've come.
So please announce us." Eventually he opened the door for us.
When we went in we found Protagoras walking in the portico
flanked by two groups. On one side were Hipponicus and his
315   brother on his mother's side, Paralus, son of Pericles, and
Charmides,[12] son of Glaucon. On the other side were Pericles'
other son, Xanthippus, Philippides, son of Philomelus, and
Antimoerus of Mende,[13] Protagoras' star pupil who is studying
professionally to become a sophist. Following behind and trying
to listen to what was being said were a group of what seemed to
be mostly foreigners, men whom Protagoras collects from the
various cities he travels through. He enchants them with his
b   voice like Orpheus, and they follow the sound of his voice in a
trance. There were some locals also in this chorus, whose dance
simply delighted me when I saw how beautifully they took care
never to get in Protagoras' way. When he turned around with
his flanking groups, the audience to the rear would split into
two in a very orderly way and then circle around to either side
and form up again behind him. It was quite lovely.

c   And then I perceived (as Homer[14] says) Hippias of Elis,[15] on a
high seat in the other side of the colonnade. Seated on benches
around him were Eryximachus,[16] son of Acoumenus, Phaedrus
of Myrrhinous, Andron,[17] son of Androtion, a number of Eleans

---

12. Charmides (d. 403 B.C.), an Athenian, brother of Plato's mother, and a leader
(along with Critias—see note 22 below) in the oligarchic revolution (of the
Thirty Tyrants) in 404. He died in the fighting during the democratic restoration.
As a young man Charmides was renowned for his beauty. Plato gives Charmides a major role in the early dialogue which bears his name.

13. Philippides, Antimoerus: faces in the crowd.

14. Homer *Odyssey* 11.601: "And then I perceived [the mighty Heracles]." Vari-
ants of this phrase are used repeatedly by Odysseus in his account of the heroes
he saw during his visit to the underworld. This allusion to Homeric epic estab-
lishes a mock-heroic tone for the scene in Callias' house.

15. Hippias of Elis, a sophist noted for his knowledge in all areas of science and
craft, ranging from mathematics and rhetoric to weaving and sewing. His dates
are uncertain, younger than Protagoras and Socrates, perhaps older than Plato.
Plato wrote two dialogues bearing his name, *Hippias Minor* and *Hippias Major*.
(The authenticity of the latter is questioned by some scholars.)

16. Eryximachus and Phaedrus. Eryximachus is a doctor. He appears in Plato's
Symposium, there as here, with his friend Phaedrus, a promising young
intellectual. Plato gives Phaedrus further attention in his later dialogue
Phaedrus.

17. Andron, another face in the crowd.

and a few other foreigners. They seemed to be asking Hippias questions on astronomy and physics, and he, from his high seat, was answering each of their questions point by point. And not only that, but I saw Tantalus[18] too, for Prodicus of Ceos[19] was also in town. He was in a room which Hipponicus had formerly used for storage, but because of the number of visitors Callias had cleared it out and made it into a guest room. Prodicus was still in bed and looked to be bundled up in a pile of sheepskin fleeces and blankets. Seated on couches next to him were Pausanias[20] from Cerames, and with Pausanias a fairly young boy, well-bred I would say, and certainly good-looking. I think I heard his name is Agathon, and I wouldn't be surprised if he were Pausanias' young love. So this boy was there, and the two Adeimantuses,[21] sons of Cepis and Leucolophidas, and there seemed to be some others. What they were talking about I couldn't tell from outside, even though I really wanted to hear Prodicus, a man who in my opinion is godlike in his universal knowledge. But his voice is so deep that it set up a reverberation in the room that blurred what was being said.

We had just arrived when along came Alcibiades the Beautiful (as you call him, and I'm not arguing) and Critias son of Call-

d

e

316

18. *Odyssey* 11.582: "And indeed I saw Tantalus suffering hardships." See note 14. There is no obvious specific point to the implied comparison between Prodicus and Tantalus, who was punished in Hades by eternal thirst and hunger though food and water were tantalizingly close. Prodicus does seem to have been in bed with a cold.

19. Prodicus of Ceos, a sophist noted for his careful distinctions of meaning among terms. His dates are uncertain; according to Plato in the *Apology*, he was alive in 399 B.C. Plato allows Socrates to say that he admires Prodicus' approach to inquiry; this expression of respect is almost certainly genuine, given Socrates' own commitment to making careful distinctions as an element of proper philosophical method. A fragment of the writing of Prodicus survives in Xenophon, *Memorabilia*; it is a moral fable on the choice of Heracles between virtue and pleasure.

20. Pausanias and Agathon: Pausanias of Cerames, a lawyer, with his friend Agathon, here a boy. Agathon, an Athenian, went on to achieve success as a tragedian. His winning of the prize at a dramatic competition (the Lenaion) in 416 B.C. was the occasion of the party which served as the dramatic setting for Plato's *Symposium*. Pausanias and Agathon both appear prominently in that dialogue.

21. the two Adeimanti: one was a general in the Peloponnesian War; the other a face in the crowd.

aeschrus.[22] So when we were inside and had spent a little more
time looking at everything, we went up to Protagoras, and
I said, "Protagoras, Hippocrates here and I have come to
see you."

"Do you want to talk with me alone or with others present?"
he said.

"It doesn't make any difference to us," I said. "Listen to what
we've come for, and decide for yourself."

"Well, then, what have you come for?" he asked.

"Hippocrates is from here, a son of Apollodoros and a member of a great and well-to-do family. His own natural ability
ranks him with the best of anyone his age. It's my impression
that he wants to be a man of respect in the city, and he thinks
this is most likely to happen if he associates himself with you.
So now you must decide. Should we talk about this alone or in
the presence of others?"

"Your discretion on my behalf is appropriate, Socrates. Caution is in order for a foreigner who goes into the great cities and
tries to persuade the best of the young men in them to abandon
their associations with others, relatives and acquaintances,
young and old alike, and to associate with him instead on the
grounds that they will be improved by this association. Jealousy,
hostility, and intrigue on a large scale are aroused by such activity. Now, I maintain that the sophist's art is an ancient one,
but that the men who practiced it in ancient times, fearing the
odium attached to it, disguised it, masking it sometimes as poetry, as Homer and Hesiod[23] and Simonides[24] did, or as mystery
religions and prophecy, witness Orpheus and Musaeus,[25] and
occasionally, I've noticed, even as athletics, as with Iccus of Tar-

---

22. Critias (c. 460–403), Athenian and cousin to Plato's mother. Critias was an
accomplished intellectual and writer of prose and poetry. Like Charmides, he
was a leader in the oligarchic tyranny of 404 and was killed in the restoration of
the democracy of 403. Critias has a major role in Plato's *Charmides*, and Plato
named a dialogue after him.

23. Hesiod was a didactic poet active in the eighth century B.C. His two princi-
pal works, *Theogony* and *Works and Days*, were fundamental texts in Greek
education and culture. Herodotus says that Homer and Hesiod gave the Greeks
their gods.

24. Simonides (c. 556–468 B.C.): a lyric and elegiac poet best known now for his
epitaph on the Spartan dead at Thermopylae.

25. Orpheus and Musaeus, two names associated with religious cults and practices at this period. Musaeus is considered to be wholly mythical. Orpheus,

entum[26] and, in our own time, Herodicus of Selymbria (originally of Megara), as great a sophist as any. Your own Agathocles,[27] a great sophist, used music as a front, as did Pythocleides of Ceos, and many others. All of them, as I say, used these various arts as screens out of fear of ill will. And this is where I part company with them all, for I do not believe that they accomplished their end; I believe they failed, in fact, to conceal from the powerful men in the cities the true purpose of their disguises. The masses, needless to say, perceive nothing, but merely sing the tune their leaders announce. Now, for a runaway not to succeed in running away, but to be caught in the open, is sheer folly from the start and inevitably makes men even more hostile than they were before, for on top of everything else they perceive him as a real rogue. So I have come down the completely opposite road. I admit that I am a sophist and that I educate men, and I consider this admission to be a better precaution than denial. And I have given thought to other precautions as well, so as to avoid, God willing, suffering any ill from admitting I am a sophist. I have been in the profession many years now, and I'm old enough to be the father of any of

317

b

c

perhaps historical, perhaps only mythical, was the famed singer whose beloved wife Eurydice died from the bite of a snake. Orpheus went to the underworld and pleaded with its ruler to allow her to live again. He was granted his plea on the condition that as he left Hades he would not turn around to look at her. He was unable to keep his promise and thence lost her forever, to his despair. Another tradition was that Orpheus was torn limb from limb by Thracian women (maenads) in a Dionysiac frenzy; yet despite this, he still lived, his severed ragged head floating down the river, singing forever sweetly.

These stories contributed to a religious cult tradition involving a cluster of beliefs, among the most prominent of which were the following: the soul was valued over the body; the body was considered as the tomb or prison of the soul; the killing of animals for food was considered as an unclean practice; such killing was also proscribed due to belief in transmigration of souls, including the souls of animals; and undergoing rites of purification (including practices of intellectual discipline) was urged for the sake of securing the good opinion of the gods and a happy existence for the soul after the separation from the body at death. These beliefs were associated also with the gods Apollo and Dionysus, as well as with the sixth-century philosopher and mathematician Pythagoras. Plato is perhaps the first and most reliable source of information about the beliefs of these cults, and he refers (favorably) to some of their doctrines in two of his dialogues, *Meno* and *Phaedo*.

26. Iccus, a sixth-century-B.C. athlete and trainer of athletes from southern Italy; Herodicus, also a famous athletic trainer, who was a physician as well.

27. Agathocles and Pythocleides, prominent musicians and music teachers.

you here. So, if you do have a request, it would give me the greatest pleasure by far to deliver my lecture in the presence of everyone in the house."

It looked to me that he wanted to show off in front of Prodicus and Hippias, and to bask in glory because we had come as his admirers, so I said, "Well, why don't we call Prodicus and Hippias over, and their companions, so that they can listen to us?"

"By all means!" said Protagoras.

"Then you want to make this a general session and have everyone take seats for a discussion?" Callias proposed this, and it seemed like the only thing to do. We were all overjoyed at the prospect of listening to wise men, and we laid hold of the benches and couches ourselves and arranged them over by Hippias, since that's where the benches were already. Meanwhile Callias and Alcibiades had gotten Prodicus up and brought him over with his group.

When we had all taken our seats, Protagoras said, "Now, then, Socrates, since these gentlemen also are present, would you please say what it was you brought up to me a little while ago on the young man's behalf."

"Well, Protagoras," I said, "as to why we have come, I'll begin as I did before. Hippocrates here has gotten to the point where he wants to be your student, and, quite naturally, he would like to know what he will get out of it if he does study with you. That's really all we have to say."

Protagoras took it from there and said, "Young man, this is what you will get if you study with me: The very day you start, you will go home a better man, and the same thing will happen the day after. Every day, day after day, you will get better and better."[28]

When I heard this I said, "What you're saying, Protagoras, isn't very surprising, but quite likely. Why, even you, though you are so old and wise, would get better if someone taught you something you didn't happen to know already. But what if the situation were a little different, and Hippocrates here all of a sudden changed his mind and set his heart on studying with this young fellow who has just come into town, Zeuxippus of

28. Protagoras' answer to the question has the quality of a catch-phrase or an advertising slogan. Recall that Socrates earlier likened a sophist to a merchant who "might deceive us in advertising what he sells" (313d).

Heraclea,[29] and came to him, as he now comes to you, and heard from him the very same thing as from you—that each day he spent with him he would become better and make progress. If Hippocrates asked him in what way he would become better, and toward what he would be making progress, Zeuxippus would say at painting. And if he were studying with Orthagoras of Thebes[30] and he heard from him the same thing as he hears from you and asked him in what he would be getting better every day he studied with him, Orthagoras would say at flute-playing. It is in this way that you must tell me and the young man on whose behalf I am asking the answer to this question: If Hippocrates studies with Protagoras, exactly how will he go away a better man and in what will he make progress each and every day he spends with you?"

Protagoras heard me out and then said, "You put your question well, Socrates, and I am only too glad to answer those who pose questions well. If Hippocrates comes to me he will not experience what he would if he studied with some other sophist. The others abuse young men, steering them back again, against their will, into subjects the likes of which they have escaped from at school, teaching them arithmetic, astronomy, geometry, music, and poetry"—at this point he gave Hippias a significant look—"but if he comes to me he will learn only what he has come for. What I teach is sound deliberation, both in domestic matters—how best to manage one's household, and in public affairs—how to realize one's maximum potential for success in political debate and action."

"Am I following what you are saying?" I asked. "You appear to be talking about the art of citizenship, and to be promising to make men good citizens."

"This is exactly what I claim, Socrates."

"Well, this is truly an admirable technique you have developed, if indeed you have. There is no point in my saying to you anything other than exactly what I think. The truth is, Protagoras, I have never thought that this could be taught, but

d

e

319

b

29. Zeuxippus (more commonly spelled Zeuxis), a painter who flourished in the late fifth century, was noted for his subtle use of color and for exceptional realism; his paintings of grapes were said to have deceived birds.

30. Orthagoras, renowned for his excellent playing on the aulos, a reed instrument played like a recorder. Aulos is traditionally translated as "flute" and is so translated later in this dialogue.

when you say it can be, I can't very well doubt it. It's only right that I explain where I got the idea that this is not teachable, not something that can be imparted from one human being to another. I maintain, along with the rest of the Greek world, that the Athenians are wise. And I observe that when we convene in the Assembly[31] and the city has to take some action on a building project, we send for builders to advise us; if it has to do with the construction of ships, we send for shipwrights; and so forth

c   for everything that is considered learnable and teachable. But if anyone else, a person not regarded as a craftsman, tries to advise them, no matter how handsome and rich and well-born he might be, they just don't accept him. They laugh at him and shout him down until he either gives up trying to speak and steps down himself, or the archer-police remove him forcibly by order of the board. This is how they proceed in matters which

d   they consider technical. But when it is a matter of deliberating on city management, anyone can stand up and advise them, carpenter, blacksmith, shoemaker, merchant, ship-captain, rich man, poor man, well-born, low-born—it doesn't matter—and nobody blasts him for presuming to give counsel without any prior training under a teacher. The reason for this is clear: They

e   do not think that this can be taught. Public life aside, the same principle holds also in private life, where the wisest and best of our citizens are unable to transmit to others the virtues that they possess. Look at Pericles,[32] the father of these young men here. He gave them a superb education in everything that

320   teachers can teach, but as for what he himself is really wise in, he neither teaches them that himself nor has anyone else teach them either, and his sons have to browse like stray sacred cattle and pick up virtue on their own wherever they might find it. Take a good look at Cleinias, the younger brother of Alcibiades here. When Pericles became his guardian he was afraid that he would be corrupted, no less, by Alcibiades. So he separated them and placed Cleinias in Ariphron's house and tried to educate him there. Six months later he gave him back to Alcibiades

31. The Athenian Assembly (ekklēsia) was, in Socrates' time, open to all male citizens over eighteen. It was the ultimate authority in the state. Debate was open, and every member had the right to speak. Voting was by simple majority. Many cases required a quorum of six thousand members.

32. Pericles (c. 495–429 B.C.), the greatest fifth-century Athenian statesman and general. He was esteemed not only for his military and civic accomplishments but also for his outstanding ability as an orator.

because he couldn't do anything with him. I could mention a   b
great many more, men who are good themselves but have never
succeeded in making anyone else better, whether family members or total strangers. Looking at these things, Protagoras, I just
don't think that virtue can be taught. But when I hear what you
have to say, I waver; I think there must be something in what
you are talking about. I consider you to be a person of enor-
mous experience who has learned much from others and
thought through a great many things for himself. So if you can
clarify for us how virtue is teachable, please don't begrudge us
your explanation."

"I wouldn't think of begrudging you an explanation, Socra-   c
tes," he replied. "But would you rather that I explain by telling
you a story, as an older man to a younger audience, or by
developing an argument?"

The consensus was that he should proceed in whichever way
he wished. "I think it would be more pleasant," he said, "if I
told you a story.

"There once was a time when the gods existed but mortal
races did not. When the time came for their appointed genesis,   d
the gods molded them inside the earth, blending together earth
and fire and various compounds of earth and fire. When they
were ready to bring them to light the gods put Prometheus and
Epimetheus[33] in charge of assigning to each its appropriate
powers and abilities.[34]

---

33. Prometheus and Epimetheus, demigods, sons of Iapetus the Titan and
Clymene. Hesiod and Aeschylus (fifth-century tragedian) are the primary
sources for our knowledge of the legends of Prometheus; Protagoras here gives
a rather different account to suit his own purposes. On the traditional accounts,
Prometheus (whose name means "fore-thinker") stole fire (which perhaps represents technological power generally) from Zeus in order to help human beings
have an easier and better life. According to Hesiod, because of this act of
Prometheus, Zeus punished all men by creating the lovely and tempting
Pandora, whose allure causes life to be difficult for men. Epimetheus (whose
name means "after-thinker") was held to be simple-minded, lacking in
cleverness, and unable to act wisely. It was he who was responsible for letting
loose all the evils and sufferings of mankind by accepting Zeus' gift of Pandora.
According to Aeschylus, Prometheus himself was horribly punished by Zeus—
he was tied to a rock, where an eagle perpetually pecked at and ate parts of his
liver.

34. The Greek term is *dunamis*, a term whose meaning is highly con-
text-dependent. Subsequent occurrences of *dunamis* translated differently are
indicated in notes below.

"Epimetheus begged Prometheus for the privilege of assigning the abilities himself. 'When I've completed the distribution,' he said, 'you can inspect it.' Prometheus agreed, and Epimetheus started distributing abilities.

"To some he assigned strength without quickness; the weaker ones he made quick. Some he armed; others he left unarmed but devised for them some other means for preserving themselves. He compensated for small size by issuing wings for flight or an underground habitat. Size was itself a safeguard for those he made large. And so on down the line, balancing his distribution, making adjustments, and taking precautions against the possible extinction of any of the races.

"After supplying them with defenses against mutual destruction, he devised for them protection against the weather. He clothed them with thick pelts and tough hides capable of warding off winter storms, effective against heat, and serving also as built-in, natural bedding when they went to sleep. He also shod them, some with hooves, others with thick pads of bloodless skin. Then he provided them with various forms of nourishment, plants for some, fruit from trees for others, roots for still others. And there were some to whom he gave the consumption of other animals as their sustenance. To some he gave the capacity for few births; to others, ravaged by the former, he gave the capacity for multiple births, and so ensured the survival of their kind.

"But Epimetheus was not very wise, and he absentmindedly used up all the powers and abilities on the nonreasoning animals; he was left with the human race, completely unequipped. While he was floundering about, at a loss, Prometheus arrived to inspect the distribution and saw that while the other animals were well provided with everything, the human race was naked, unshod, unbedded, and unarmed, and it was already the day on which all of them, human beings included, were destined to emerge from the earth into the light. It was then that Prometheus, desperate to find some means of survival for the human race, stole from Hephaestus and Athena[35] wisdom in the

---

35. Athena, patron goddess of Athens. The special areas of her power referred to here were the arts of warfare and the more docile arts and crafts of weaving, spinning, smithing, and potting. Hephaestus, god of fire and also of the craft of smithing and technological invention, was especially honored in urban areas, where these crafts were most highly developed.

practical arts together with fire (without which this kind of wisdom is effectively useless) and gave them outright to the human race. The wisdom it acquired was for staying alive; wisdom for living together in society, political wisdom, it did not acquire, because that was in the keeping of Zeus. Prometheus no longer had free access to the high citadel that is the house of Zeus, and besides this, the guards there were terrifying. But he did sneak into the building that Athena and   e
Hephaestus shared to practice their arts, and he stole from Hephaestus the art of fire and from Athena her arts, and he gave them to the human race. And it is from this origin that the   322
resources human beings needed to stay alive came into being. Later, the story goes, Prometheus was charged with theft, all on account of Epimetheus.

"It is because humans had a share of the divine dispensation that they alone among animals worshipped the gods, with whom they had a kind of kinship, and erected altars and sacred images. It wasn't long before they were articulating speech and words and had invented houses, clothes, shoes, and blankets, and were nourished by food from the earth. Thus equipped,   b
human beings at first lived in scattered isolation; there were no cities. They were being destroyed by wild beasts because they were weaker in every way, and although their technology was adequate to obtain food, it was deficient when it came to fighting wild animals. This was because they did not yet possess the art of politics, of which the art of war is a part. They did indeed try to band together and survive by founding cities. The outcome when they did so was that they wronged each other, because they did not possess the art of politics, and so they would scatter and again be destroyed. Zeus was afraid that our   c
whole race might be wiped out, so he sent Hermes[36] to bring justice and a sense of shame to humans, so that there would be order within cities and bonds of friendship to unite them. Hermes asked Zeus how he should distribute shame and justice to humans. 'Should I distribute them as the other arts were? This is how the others were distributed: one person practicing the art of medicine suffices for many ordinary people; and so forth with the other practitioners. Should I establish justice and

---

36. Hermes, god of communication between realms—from gods to men, and the guide of souls of men to the netherworld; he was also associated with fertility and impudent clever pranks.

d   shame among humans in this way, or distribute it to all?' 'To all,'
           said Zeus, 'and let all have a share. For cities would never come
           to be if only a few possessed these, as is the case with the other
           arts. And establish this law as coming from me: Death to him
           who cannot partake of shame and justice, for he is a pestilence
           to the city.'
              "And so it is, Socrates, that when the Athenians (and others
           as well) are debating architectural excellence, or the virtue
           proper to any other professional specialty, they think that only a
           few individuals have the right to advise them, and they do not
e   accept advice from anyone outside these select few. You've made
           this point yourself, and with good reason, I might add. But
           when the debate involves political excellence, which must pro-
323   ceed entirely from justice and temperance, they accept advice
           from anyone, and with good reason, for they think that this
           particular virtue, political or civic virtue, is shared by all, or
           there wouldn't be any cities. This must be the explanation for it,
           Socrates.
              "And so you won't think you've been deceived, consider this
           as further evidence for the universal belief that all humans have
           a share of justice and the rest of civic virtue. In the other arts, as
           you have said, if someone claims to be a good flute-player or
           whatever, but is not, people laugh at him or get angry with him,
b   and his family comes round and remonstrates with him as if he
           were mad. But when it comes to justice or any other social
           virtue, even if they know someone is unjust, if that person pub-
           licly confesses the truth about himself, they will call this truth-
           fulness madness, whereas in the previous case they would have
           called it a sense of decency. They will say that everyone ought to
c   claim to be just, whether they are or not, and that it is madness
           not to pretend to justice, since one must have some trace of it or
           not be human.
              "This, then, is my first point: It is reasonable to admit every-
           one as an adviser on this virtue, on the grounds that everyone
           has some share of it. Next I will attempt to show that people do
           not regard this virtue as natural or self-generated, but as some-
           thing taught and carefully developed in those in whom it is
           developed.
d   "In the case of evils that men universally regard as afflictions
           due to nature or bad luck, no one ever gets angry with anyone
           so afflicted or reproves, admonishes, punishes, or tries to cor-
           rect them. We simply pity them. No one in his right mind would

try to do anything like this to someone who is ugly, for example, or scrawny or weak. The reason is, I assume, that they know that these things happen to people as a natural process or by chance, both these ills and their opposites. But in the case of the good things that accrue to men through practice and training and teaching, if someone does not possess these goods but rather their corresponding evils, he finds himself the object of anger, punishment, and reproof. Among these evils are injustice, impiety, and in general everything that is opposed to civic virtue. Offenses in this area are always met with anger and reproof, and the reason is clearly that this virtue is regarded as something acquired through practice and teaching. The key, Socrates, to the true significance of punishment lies in the fact that human beings consider virtue to be something acquired through training. For no one punishes a wrong-doer in consideration of the simple fact that he has done wrong, unless one is exercising the mindless vindictiveness of a beast. Reasonable punishment is not vengeance for a past wrong—for one cannot undo what has been done—but is undertaken with a view to the future, to deter both the wrong-doer and whoever sees him being punished from repeating the crime. This attitude towards punishment as deterrence implies that virtue is learned, and this is the attitude of all those who seek requital in public or in private. All human beings seek requital from and punish those who they think have wronged them, and the Athenians, your fellow citizens, especially do so. Therefore, by my argument, the Athenians are among those who think that virtue is acquired and taught. So it is with good reason that your fellow citizens accept a blacksmith's or a cobbler's advice in political affairs. And they do think that virtue is acquired and taught. It appears to me that both these propositions have been sufficiently proved, Socrates.

"Now, on to your remaining difficulty, the problem you raise about good men teaching their sons everything that can be taught and making them wise in these subjects, but not making them better than anyone else in the particular virtue in which they themselves excel. On this subject, Socrates, I will abandon story for argument. Consider this: Does there or does there not exist one thing which all citizens must have for there to be a city? Here and nowhere else lies the solution to your problem. For if such a thing exists, and this one thing is not the art of the carpenter, the blacksmith, or the potter, but justice, and tem-

325 perance, and piety—what I may collectively term the virtue of a man, and if this is the thing which everyone should share in and with which every man should act whenever he wants to learn anything or do anything, but should not act without it, and if we should instruct and punish those who do
b not share in it, man, woman, and child, until their punishment makes them better, and should exile from our cities or execute whoever doesn't respond to punishment and instruction; if this is the case, if such is the nature of this thing, and good men give their sons an education in everything but this, then we have to be amazed at how strangely our good men behave. For we have shown that they regard this thing as teachable both in private and public life. Since it is something that can be taught and nurtured, is it possible that they have their sons taught everything in which there is no death penalty for not understanding it, but when their children are faced with the death penalty or
c exile if they fail to learn virtue and be nurtured in it—and not only death but confiscation of property and, practically speaking, complete familial catastrophe—do you think they do not have them taught this or give them all the attention possible? We must think that they do, Socrates.

"Starting when they are little children and continuing as long as they live, they teach them and correct them. As soon as a
d child understands what is said to him, the nurse, mother, tutor, and the father himself fight for him to be as good as he possibly can, seizing on every action and word to teach him and show him that this is just, that is unjust, this is noble, that is ugly, this is pious, that is impious, he should do this, he should not do that. If he obeys willingly, fine; if not, they straighten him out with threats and blows as if he were a twisted, bent piece of wood. After this they send him to school and tell his teachers to
e pay more attention to his good conduct than to his grammar or music lessons. The teachers pay attention to these things, and when the children have learned their letters and are getting to understand writing as well as the spoken language, they are given the works of good poets to read at their desks and have to
326 learn them by heart, works that contain numerous exhortations, many passages describing in glowing terms good men of old, so that the child is inspired to imitate them and become like them. In a similar vein, the music teachers too foster in their young pupils a sense of moral decency and restraint, and when they learn to play the lyre they are taught the works of still more

good poets, the lyric and choral poets. The teachers arrange the   b
scores and drill the rhythms and scales into the children's souls,
so that they become gentler, and their speech and movements
become more rhythmical and harmonious. For all of human life
requires a high degree of rhythm and harmony. On top of all
this, they send their children to an athletic trainer so that they
may have sound bodies in the service of their now fit minds and
will not be forced to cowardice in war or other activities through   c
physical deficiencies.

"This is what the most able, i.e., the richest, do. Their sons
start going to school at the earliest age and quit at the latest age.
And when they quit school, the city in turn compels them to   d
learn the laws and to model their lives on them. They are not to
act as they please. An analogy might be drawn from the practice
of writing-teachers, who sketch the letters faintly with a pen in
workbooks for their beginning students and have them write
the letters over the patterns they have drawn. In the same way
the city has drawn up laws invented by the great lawgivers in
the past and compels them to govern and be governed by them.
She punishes anyone who goes beyond these laws, and the
term for this punishment in your city and others is, because it is
a corrective legal action, 'correction.'   e

"When so much care and attention is paid to virtue, Socrates,
both in public and private, are you still puzzled about virtue
being teachable? The wonder would be if it were not teachable.

"Why, then, do many sons of good fathers never amount to
anything? I want you to understand this too, and in fact it's no
great wonder, if what I've just been saying is true about virtue
being something in which no one can be a layman if there is to   327
be a city. For if what I am saying is true—and nothing could be
more true: Pick any other pursuit or study and reflect upon it.
Suppose, for instance, there could be no city unless we were all
flute-players, each to the best of his ability, and everybody were
teaching everybody else this art in public and private and repri-
manding the poor players and doing all this unstintingly, just as
now no one begrudges or conceals his expertise in what is just   b
and lawful as he does his other professional expertise. For it is
to our collective advantage that we each possess justice and
virtue, and so we all gladly tell and teach each other what is just
and lawful. Well, if we all had the same eagerness and gener-
osity in teaching each other flute-playing, do you think, Socrates, that the sons of good flute-players would be more likely to

be good flute-players than the sons of poor flute-players? I don't think so at all. When a son happened to be naturally disposed toward flute-playing, he would progress and become famous; otherwise, he would remain obscure. In many cases the son of a good player would turn out to be a poor one, and the son of a poor player would turn out to be good. But as flute-players, they would all turn out to be capable when compared with ordinary people who had never studied the flute. Likewise you must regard the most unjust person ever reared in a human society under law as a paragon of justice compared with people lacking education and lawcourts and the pervasive pressure to cultivate virtue, savages such as the playwright Pherecrates[37] brought on stage at last year's Lenaion. There's no doubt that if you found yourself among such people, as did the misanthropes in that play's chorus, you would be delighted to meet up with the likes of Eurybatus and Phrynondas[38] and would sorely miss the immorality of the people here. As it is, Socrates, you affect delicate sensibilities, because everyone here is a teacher of virtue, to the best of his ability, and you can't see a single one. You might as well look for a teacher of Greek; you wouldn't find a single one of those either. Nor would you be any more successful if you asked who could teach the sons of our craftsmen the very arts which they of course learned from their fathers, to the extent that their fathers were competent, and their friends in the trade. It would be difficult to produce someone who could continue their education, whereas it would be easy to find a teacher for the totally unskilled. It is the same with virtue and everything else. If there is someone who is the least bit more advanced in virtue than ourselves, he is to be cherished.

"I consider myself to be such a person, uniquely qualified to assist others in becoming noble and good, and worth the fee that I charge and even more, so much so that even my students agree. This is why I charge according to the following system: a student pays the full price only if he wishes to; otherwise, he goes into a temple, states under oath how much he thinks my lessons are worth, and pays that amount.

"There you have it, Socrates, my mythic story and my argu-

37. Pherecrates, an Athenian writer of comic plays and prize-winner at the Lenaion dramatic competition in the late fifth century.

38. Eurybatus and Phrynondas, historical individuals, whose names had in literature become synonymous with viciousness.

ment that virtue is teachable and that the Athenians consider it
to be so, and that it is no wonder that worthless sons are born of
good fathers and good sons of worthless fathers, since even the
sons of Polycleitus,[39] of the same age as Paralus and Xanthippus
here, are nothing compared to their father, and the same is true   d
for the sons of other artisans. But it is not fair to accuse these
two yet; there is still hope for them, for they are young."
       Protagoras ended his virtuoso performance here and stopped
speaking. I was entranced and just looked at him for a long time
as if he were going to say more. I was still eager to listen, but
when I perceived that he had really stopped I pulled myself
together and, looking at Hippocrates, barely managed to say:
"Son of Apollodorus, how grateful I am to you for suggesting   e
that I come here. It is marvelous to have heard from Protagoras
what I have just heard. Formerly I used to think there was no
human practice by which the good become good, but now I am
persuaded that there is, except for one small obstacle which
Protagoras will explain away, I am sure, since he has explained
away so much already. Now, you could hear a speech similar to   329
this from Pericles or some other competent orator if you happened to be present when one of them was speaking on this
subject. But try asking one of them something, and they will be
as unable to answer your question or to ask one of their own as
a book would be. Question the least little thing in their speeches
and they will go on like bronze bowls that keep ringing for a
long time after they have been struck and prolong the sound
indefinitely unless you dampen them. That's how these orators
are: Ask them one little question and they're off on another   b
long-distance speech. But Protagoras here, while perfectly capable of delivering a beautiful long speech, as we have just seen, is
also able to reply briefly when questioned, and to put a question
and then wait for and accept the answer—rare accomplishments
these.
       "Now, then, Protagoras, I need one little thing, and then I'll
have it all, if you'll just answer me this. You say that virtue is
teachable, and if there's any human being who could persuade
me of this, it's you. But there is one thing you said that troubles   c
me, and maybe you can satisfy my soul. You said that Zeus sent
justice and a sense of shame to the human race. You also said, at

39. See n. 8.

many points in your speech, that justice and temperance[40] and piety and all these things were somehow collectively one thing: virtue. Could you go through this again and be more precise? Is virtue a single thing, with justice and temperance and piety its parts, or are the things I have just listed all names for a single entity? This is what still intrigues me."

"This is an easy question to answer, Socrates," he replied. "Virtue is a single entity, and the things you are asking about are its parts."

"Parts as in the parts of a face: mouth, nose, eyes, and ears? Or parts as in the parts of gold, where there is no difference, except for size, between parts or between the parts and the whole?"

"In the former sense, I would think, Socrates: as the parts of the face are to the whole face."

"Then tell me this. Do some people have one part and some another, or do you necessarily have all the parts if you have any one of them?"

"By no means, since many are courageous but unjust, and many again are just but not wise."

"Then these also are parts of virtue—wisdom and courage?"

"Absolutely, and wisdom is the greatest part."

"Is each of them different from the others?"

"Yes."

"And does each also have its own unique power or function?[41] In the analogy to the parts of the face, the eye is not like the ear, nor is its power or function the same, and this applies to the other parts as well: They are not like each other in power or function or in any other way. Is this how it is with the parts of virtue? Are they unlike each other, both in themselves and in their powers or functions? Is it not clear that this must be the case, if our analogy is valid?"

"Yes, it must be the case, Socrates."

"Then, none of the other parts of virtue is like knowledge, or like justice, or like courage, or like temperance, or like piety?"

---

40. The Greek term is *sōphrosunē*. For Plato, *sōphrosunē* was a complex virtue involving self-control and moderation of the physical appetites, as well as self-knowledge. There is no exact synonym in English for the full range of meanings of *sōphrosunē* in the philosophical context. Plato's *Charmides* is a dialogue devoted to inquiring into the nature and value of *sōphrosunē*.

41. *dunamis*, here best translated "power or function."

"Agreed."

"Come on, then, and let's consider together what kind of thing each of these is. Here's a good first question: Is justice a thing or is it not a thing? I think it is. What about you?"

"I think so too."

"The next step, then: Suppose someone asked us, 'Protagoras and Socrates, tell me about this thing you just named, justice. Is it itself just or unjust?' My answer would be that it is just. What would your verdict be? The same as mine or different?"

"The same."

"Then justice is the sort of thing that is just. That's how I would reply to the questioner. Would you also?"

"Yes."

"Suppose he questioned us further: 'Do you also say there is a thing called piety?' We would say we do, right?"

"Right."

"'Do you say this too is a thing?' We would say we do, wouldn't we?"

"That too."

"'Do you say that this thing is by nature impious or pious?' Myself, I would be irritated with this question and would say, 'Quiet, man! How could anything else be pious if piety itself is not?' What about you? Wouldn't you answer in the same way?"

"Absolutely."

"Suppose he asked us next: 'Then what about what you said a little while ago? Maybe I didn't hear you right. I thought you two said that the parts of virtue are related to each other in such a way that no part resembles any other.' I would answer, 'There's nothing wrong with your hearing, except that I didn't say that. Protagoras here said that in answer to my question.' If he were to say then, 'Is he telling the truth, Protagoras? Are you the one who says that one part of virtue is not like another? Is this dictum yours?' how would you answer him?"

"I would have to admit it, Socrates."

"Well, if we accept that, Protagoras, what are we going to say if he asks next, 'Isn't piety the sort of thing that is just, and isn't justice the sort of thing that is pious? Or is it the sort of thing which is not pious? Is piety the sort of thing to be not just, and therefore unjust, and justice impious?' What are we going to say to him? Personally, I would answer both that justice is pious and piety is just, and I would give the same answer on your behalf (if you would let me), that justice is the same thing as piety, or very similar, and, most emphatically, that justice is the same kind of thing as piety, and piety as justice. What do you think? Will you veto this answer, or are you in agreement with it?"

c   "It's not so absolutely clear a case to me, Socrates, as to make me grant that justice is pious, and piety just. It seems a distinction is in order here. But what's the difference? If you want, we'll let justice be pious and piety just."

"Don't do that to me! It's not this 'if you want' or 'if you agree' business I want to test. It's you and me I want to put on the line, and I think the argument will be tested best if we take the 'if' out."

d   "Well, all right. Justice does have some resemblance to piety. Anything at all resembles any other thing in some way. There is a certain way in which white resembles black, and hard soft, and so on for all the usual polar opposites. And the things we were just talking about as having different powers or functions and not being the same kinds of things—the parts of the face—

e   these resemble each other in a certain way, and they are like each other. So by this method you could prove, if you wanted to, that these things too are all like each other. But it's not right to call things similar because they resemble each other in some way, however slight, or to call them dissimilar because there is some slight point of dissimilarity."

I was taken aback, and said to him, "Do you consider the relationship between justice and piety really only one of some slight similarity?"

332   "Not exactly, but not what you seem to think it is either."

"Well, then, since you seem to me to be annoyed about this, let's drop it and consider another point that you raised. Do you acknowledge that there is such a thing as folly?"

"Yes."

"And diametrically opposed to it is wisdom?"

"It seems so to me."

"And when people act correctly and beneficially, do they seem to you to be acting temperately or the opposite?"

"Temperately."

"Then it is by virtue of temperance that they are temperate?"

b   "It has to be."

"And those who do not act correctly act foolishly, and those who act this way are not temperate?"[42]

"I agree."

"And the opposite of acting foolishly is acting temperately?"

"Yes."

"And foolish behavior comes from folly, just as temperate behavior comes from temperance?"

"Yes."

"And if something is done with strength, it is done strongly; if done with weakness, it is done weakly?"

"I agree."

"If it is done with quickness, it is done quickly, and if with slowness, slowly?"

"Yes."

"So whatever is done in a certain way is done through the   c
agency of a certain quality, and whatever is done in the opposite way is done through the agency of its opposite?"

"I agree."

"Then let's go on. Is there such a thing as beauty?"

"Yes."

"Is there any opposite to it except ugliness?"

"There is not."

"Is there such a thing as goodness?"

"There is."

"Is there any opposite to it except badness?"

"There is not."

"Is there such a thing as a shrill tone?"

"There is."

"Is there any opposite to it except a deep tone?"

"No, there is not."

"So for each thing that can have an opposite, there is only one   d
opposite, not many?"

"I agree."

"Suppose we now count up our points of agreement. Have we agreed that there is one opposite for one thing, and no more?"

"Yes, we have."

"And that what is done in an opposite way is done through the agency of opposites?"

---

42. The pair of nouns "folly/temperance" translate the Greek pair *aphrosunē/sōphrosunē*.

"Yes."

"And have we agreed that what is done foolishly is done in a way opposite to what is done temperately?"

"We have."

"And that what is done temperately is done through temperance, and what is done foolishly is done through folly?"

"Agreed."

e   "And it's true that if it's done in an opposite way, it is done through the agency of an opposite?"

"Yes."

"And one is done through temperance, the other through folly?"

"Yes."

"In an opposite way?"

"Yes."

"Through opposing agencies?"

"Yes."

"Then folly is the opposite of temperance?"

"It seems so."

"Well, then, do you recall our previous agreement that folly is the opposite of wisdom?"

"Yes, I do."

"And that one thing has only one opposite?"

"Of course."

333   "Then which of these propositions should we abandon, Protagoras? The proposition that for one thing there is only one opposite, or the one stating that wisdom is different from temperance and that each is a part of virtue, and that in addition to being distinct they are dissimilar, both in themselves and in their powers or functions, just like the parts of a face? Which should we abandon? The two statements are dissonant; they are not in harmony with one another. How could they be, if there is

b   one and only one opposite for each single thing, while folly, which is a single thing, evidently has two opposites, wisdom and temperance? Isn't this how it stands, Protagoras?"

He assented, although very grudgingly, and I continued: "Wouldn't that make wisdom and temperance one thing? And a little while ago it looked like justice and piety were nearly the same thing. Come on, Protagoras, we can't quit now, not before we've tied up these loose ends. So, does someone who acts unjustly seem temperate to you in that he acts unjustly?"

"I would be ashamed to say that is so, Socrates, although   c
many people do say it."

"Then shall I address myself to them or to you?"

"If you like, why don't you debate the majority position first?"

"It makes no difference to me, provided you give the answers,
whether it is your own opinion or not. I am primarily interested
in testing the argument, although it may happen both that the
questioner, myself, and my respondent wind up being tested."

At first Protagoras played it coy, claiming the argument was   d
too hard for him to handle, but after a while he consented to
answer.

"Let's start all over, then," I said, "with this question. Do you
think some people are being sensible[43] when they act unjustly?"

"Let us grant it," he said.

"And by 'sensible' you mean having good sense?"

"Yes."

"And having good sense means having good judgment in
acting unjustly?"

"Granted."

"Whether or not they get good results by acting unjustly?"

"Only if they get good results."

"Are you saying, then, that there are things that are good?"

"I am."

"These good things constitute what is advantageous to
people?"

"Good God, yes! And even if they are not advantageous to   e
people, I can still call them good."

I could see that Protagoras was really worked up and strug-
gling by now and that he was dead set against answering
any more. Accordingly, I carefully modified the tone of my
questions.

"Do you mean things that are advantageous to no human   334
being, Protagoras, or things that are of no advantage what-
soever? Do you call things like that good?"

"Of course not," he said. "But I know of many things that are
disadvantageous to humans, foods and drinks and drugs and
many other things, and some that are advantageous; some that
are neither to humans but one or the other to horses; some that

---

43. The Greek term is *sōphronein*, a verb related to the noun *sōphrosunē*. See the
note at 329c.

are advantageous only to cattle; some only to dogs; some that
are advantageous to none of these but are so to trees; some that
b   are good for the roots of a tree, but bad for its shoots, such as
manure, which is good spread on the roots of any plant but
absolutely ruinous if applied to the new stems and branches. Or
take olive oil, which is extremely bad for all plants and is the
worst enemy of the hair of all animals except humans, for
whose hair it is beneficial, as it is for the rest of their bodies. But
the good is such a multifaceted and variable thing that, in the
c   case of oil, it is good for the external parts of the human body
but very bad for the internal parts, which is why doctors universally forbid their sick patients to use oil in their diets except for
the least bit, just enough to dispel a prepared meal's unappetiz-
ing aroma."

When the applause for this speech of Protagoras had died
down, I said, "Protagoras, I tend to be a forgetful sort of person,
d   and if someone speaks to me at length I tend to forget the
subject of the speech. Now, if I happened to be hard of hearing
and you were going to converse with me, you would think you
had better speak louder to me than to others. In the same way,
now that you have fallen in with a forgetful person, you will
have to cut your answers short if I am going to follow you."

"How short are you ordering me to make my answers?
Shorter than necessary?"

"By no means."

"As long as necessary?"

e   "Yes."

"Then should I answer at the length I think necessary or the
length you think necessary?"

"Well, I have heard, anyway, that when you are instructing
someone in a certain subject, you are able to speak at length, if
335   you choose, and never get off the subject, or to speak so briefly
that no one could be briefer. So if you are going to converse
with me, please use the latter form of expression, brevity."

"Socrates, I have had verbal contests with many people, and if
I were to accede to your request and do as my opponent de-
manded, I would not be thought superior to anyone, nor would
Protagoras be a name to be reckoned with among the Greeks."

I could see he was uncomfortable with his previous answers
b   and that he would no longer be willing to go on answering in a
dialectical discussion, so I considered my work with him to be
finished, and I said so: "You know, Protagoras, I'm not exactly

pleased myself that our session has not gone the way you think it should. But if you are ever willing to hold a discussion in such a way that I can follow, I will participate in it with you. People say of you—and you say yourself—that you are able to discuss things speaking either at length or briefly. You are a wise man,   c after all. But I don't have the ability to make those long speeches: I only wish I did. It was up to you, who have the ability to do both, to make this concession, so that the discussion could have had a chance. But since you're not willing, and I'm somewhat busy and unable to stay for your extended speeches—there's somewhere I have to go—I'll be leaving now. Although I'm sure it would be rather nice to hear them."

Having had my say, I stood up as if to go, but as I was getting   d up, Callias took hold of my wrist with his right hand and grasped this cloak I'm wearing with his left. "We won't let you go, Socrates," he said. "Our discussions wouldn't be the same without you, so please stay here with us, I beg you. There's nothing I would rather hear than you and Protagoras in debate. Please do us all a favor."

By now I was on my feet and really making as if to leave. I said, "Son of Hipponicus, I have always admired your love of   e wisdom, and I especially honor and hold it dear now. I would be more than willing to gratify you, if you would ask me something that is possible for me. As it is, you might as well be asking me to keep up with Crison of Himera, the champion sprinter,[44] or to compete with the distance runners, or match strides with the couriers who run all day long. What could I say, except that I want it for myself more than you want it for me, but I simply cannot match these runners' pace, and if you want   336 to watch me running in the same race with Crison, you must ask him to slow down to my speed, since I am not able to run fast, but he is able to run slowly. So if you have your heart set on hearing me and Protagoras, you must ask him to answer my questions now as he did at the outset—briefly. If he doesn't, what turn will our dialogue take? To me, the mutual exchange of   b a dialogue is something quite distinct from a public address."

---

44. Crison of Himera was the Olympic champion in the stade run (two hundred meters) in 448, 444, and 440 B.C. Long-distance couriers (*hemerodromoi*, day-runners) were able to cover approximately seventy-five miles a day. The best known is Pheidippides, who ran from Athens to Sparta (one hundred fifty miles) in two days (Herodotus, vi. 105).

"But you see, Socrates, Protagoras has a point when he says that he ought to be allowed, no less than you, to conduct the discussion as he sees fit."

At this point Alcibiades jumped in and said: "You're not making sense, Callias. Socrates admits that long speeches are beyond him and concedes to Protagoras on that score. But when it comes to dialectical discussion and understanding the give and take of argument, I would be surprised if he yields to anyone. Now, if Protagoras admits that he is Socrates' inferior in dialectic, that should be enough for Socrates. But if he contests the point, let him engage in a question-and-answer dialogue and not spin out a long speech every time he answers, fending off the issues because he doesn't want to be accountable, and going on and on until most of the listeners have forgotten what the question was about, although I guarantee you Socrates won't forget, no matter how he jokes about his memory. So I think that Socrates has a stronger case. Each of us ought to make clear his own opinion."

After Alcibiades it was Critias, I think, who spoke next: "Well, Prodicus and Hippias, it seems to me that Callias is very much on Protagoras' side, while Alcibiades as usual wants to be on the winning side of a good fight. But there's no need for any of us to lend partisan support to either Socrates or Protagoras. We should instead join in requesting them both not to break up our meeting prematurely."

Prodicus spoke up next: "That's well said, Critias. Those who attend discussions such as this ought to listen impartially, but not equally, to both interlocutors. There is a distinction here. We ought to listen impartially but not divide our attention equally: More should go to the wiser speaker and less to the more unlearned. For my part, I think that the two of you ought to debate the issues, but dispense with eristics. Friends debate each other on good terms; eristics are for enemies at odds. In this way our meeting would take a most attractive turn, for you, the speakers, would then most surely earn the respect, rather than the praise, of those of us listening to you. For respect is guilelessly inherent in the souls of the listeners, but praise is all too often merely a deceitful verbal expression. And then, too, we, your audience, would be most cheered, but not pleased, for to be cheered is to learn something, to participate in some intellectual activity, and is a mental state; but to be pleased has to do with eating or experiencing some other pleasure in one's body."

Prodicus' remarks were enthusiastically received by the majority of us, and then the wise Hippias spoke: "Gentlemen, I regard all of you here present as kinsmen, intimates, and fellow citizens by nature, not by convention. For like is akin to like by nature, but convention, which tyrannizes the human race, often constrains us contrary to nature. Therefore it would be disgraceful for us to understand the nature of things and not—being as we are the wisest of the Greeks and gathered here together in this veritable hall of wisdom, in this greatest and most august house of the city itself—not, I say, produce anything worthy of all this dignity, but bicker with each other as if we were the dregs of society. I therefore implore and counsel you, Protagoras and Socrates, to be reconciled and to compromise, under our arbitration, as it were, on some middle course. You, Socrates, must not insist on that precise, excessively brief form of discussion if it does not suit Protagoras, but rather allow free rein to the speeches, so that they might communicate to us more impressively and elegantly. And you, Protagoras, must not let out full sail in the wind and leave the land behind to disappear into the Sea of Rhetoric. Both of you must steer a middle course. So that's what you shall do, and take my advice and choose a referee or moderator or supervisor who will monitor for you the length of your speeches."

Everyone there thought this was a fine idea and gave it their approval. Callias said he wouldn't let me go, and they requested me to choose a moderator. I said it would be unseemly to choose someone to umpire our speeches. "If the person chosen is going to be our inferior, it is not right for an inferior to supervise his superiors. If he's our peer that's no good either, because he will do the same as we would and be superfluous. Choose someone who's our superior? I honestly think it's impossible for you to choose someone wiser than Protagoras. And if you choose someone who is not his superior but claim that he is, then you're insulting him. Protagoras is just not the insignificant sort of person for whom you appoint a supervisor. For myself, I don't care one way or another. But you have your heart set on this conference and these discussions proceeding, and if that's going to happen, this is what I want to do. If Protagoras is not willing to answer questions, let him ask them, and I will answer, and at the same time I will try to show him how I think the answerer ought to answer. When I've answered all the questions he wishes to ask, then it's his turn to be accountable to me in the same way. So if he doesn't seem ready and willing to answer the actual question asked, you and I will unite in urgently requesting him, as you have requested me, not to ruin

e   our conference. This will not require any one supervisor, since you will all supervise together."

Everyone agreed this was the thing to do. Protagoras wanted no part of it, but he had to agree to ask questions, and when he had asked enough, to respond in turn with short answers.

So he began to ask questions something like this: "I consider,

339   Socrates, that the greatest part of a man's education is to be in command of poetry, by which I mean the ability to understand the words of the poets, to know when a poem is correctly composed and when not, and to know how to analyze a poem and to respond to questions about it. So my line of questioning now will still concern the subject of our present discussion, namely virtue, but translated into the sphere of poetry. Now, Simonides[45] somewhere says to Scopas, the son of Creon of Thessaly:

b   *For a man to become good truly is hard,*
in hands and feet and mind foursquare,
blamelessly built . . .

Do you know this lyric ode, or shall I recite it all for you?"

I told him there was no need, for I knew the poem, and it happened to be one to which I had given especially careful attention.

"Good," he said. "So, do you think it's well made or not?"

"Very well made."

"And do you think it's well made if the poet contradicts himself?"

"No."

---

45. The meaning and purpose of the ode by Simonides under discussion here has been the subject of considerable scholarly debate. The general view is that Simonides, influenced by democratic ideas, is redefining the terms *agathos* and *esthlos*. Both these words mean "good" in a general sense and are so translated here. But both terms also carried strong connotations of aristocratic, upper-class values. For Pittacus (see n. 46) the phrase *esthlos aner*, "good man," meant a noble, an aristocrat who embodied all of the values of his social class. Simonides is suggesting that what it means to be a good man is not wealth, noble birth, physical strength, or political power, but competence in useful work, avoidance of bad conduct, and a sense of justice. This is not, however, how Plato has Socrates interpret the poem.

"Take a better look then."   c
"As I've said, I'm already familiar enough with it."
"Then you must know that at some point later in the ode he says:

> Nor is Pittacus'[46] proverb in tune
> however wise a man he was.
> Hard it is to be good, he said.

"You do recognize that both these things are said by the same person?"
"I do."
"Well, do you think that the latter is consistent with the former?"
"It seems so to me," I said (but as I said it I was afraid he had a point there). "Doesn't it seem so to you?"
"How can anyone who says both these things be consistent?   d
First, he asserts himself that it is hard for a man truly to become good, and then, a little further on in his poem he forgets and criticizes Pittacus for saying the same thing as he did, that it is hard for a man to be good, and refuses to accept from him the same thing that he himself said. And yet, when he criticizes him for saying the same thing as himself, he obviously criticizes himself as well, so either the earlier or the later must not be right."

Protagoras got a noisy round of applause for this speech. At first I felt as if I had been hit by a good boxer. Everything went   e
black and I was reeling from Protagoras' oratory and the others' clamor. Then, to tell you the truth, to stall for time to consider what the poet meant, I turned to Prodicus and, calling on him, "Prodicus," I said, "Simonides was from your hometown, wasn't he? It's your duty to come to the man's rescue, so I don't mind   340
calling for your help, just as Homer says Scamander called Simois to help him when he was besieged by Achilles:

> Dear brother, let's buck this hero's strength together.[47]

So also do I summon your aid, lest to our dismay Protagoras destroy Simonides. But really, Prodicus, Simonides' rehabilita-

---

46. Pittacus (650–570 B.C.), ruler of Mytilene and often considered one of the Seven Sages (for which see n. 51). The context of Pittacus' dictum "It is hard to be good (*esthlos*)" is that he said it when, already advanced in years, he was obliged to lead his troops in battle.
47. Homer, *Iliad* 21.308.

b tion does require your special art, by which you distinguish 'wanting' from 'desiring' and make all the other fine distinctions that you did just a while ago. So tell me if you agree with me, because it's not clear to me that Simonides does in fact contradict himself. Just give us your offhand opinion. Are becoming and being the same or different?"

"Good heavens, different."

"All right. Now, in the first passage, Simonides declared as his own opinion that it is hard for a man truly to become good."

c "That's right," Prodicus said.

"Then he criticizes Pittacus not for saying the same thing as himself, as Protagoras thinks, but for saying something different. Because Pittacus did not say that it is hard to *become* good, as Simonides said, but to *be* good. As Prodicus here says, being and becoming are not the same thing, Protagoras. And if

d being is not the same as becoming, Simonides does not contradict himself. Perhaps Prodicus and many others might agree with Hesiod that it is difficult to become good:

> The gods put Goodness where we have to sweat
> To get at her. But once you reach the top
> She's as easy to have as she was hard at first."[48]

Prodicus applauded me when he heard this, but Protagoras said, "Your rehabilitation, Socrates, has a crippling error greater than the one you are correcting."

"Then I've done my work badly," I said, "and I am the ridiculous sort of physician whose cure is worse than the disease."

"That's exactly right," he said.

e "How so?" said I.

"The poet's ignorance would be monumental if he says the possession of virtue is so trivial when everyone agrees it is the hardest thing in the world."

Then I said, "By heaven, Prodicus' participation in our discussion couldn't be more timely. It may well be, Protagoras, that

341 Prodicus' wisdom is of ancient and divine origin, dating back to the time of Simonides or even earlier. But although your experience is very broad, it does not seem to extend to this branch of

---

48. Hesiod, *Works and Days* 289, 291–92. "Goodness" here is translating the Greek *aretē*. Hesiod preceded Simonides in identifying goodness not with social class but with correct behavior.

wisdom, which I have been schooled in as a pupil of Prodicus. And now it appears that you do not understand that Simonides may well have not conceived of the word 'hard'[49] as you do. In much the same way Prodicus corrects me each time I use the word 'terrible'[50] to praise you or someone else, as, for example, 'Protagoras is a terribly wise man.' When I say that, he asks me if I am not ashamed to call good things terrible. For terrible, he says, is bad. No one ever speaks of terrible wealth, or terrible peace, or terrible well-being, but we do hear of terrible disease, terrible war, and terrible poverty, 'terrible' here being 'bad.' So perhaps the Ceans and Simonides conceived of 'hard' as 'bad' or something else that you do not understand. Let's ask Prodicus. He's just the right person to consult on Simonides' dialect. Prodicus, what did Simonides mean by 'hard'?"

" 'Bad.' "

"Then this is why he criticizes Pittacus for saying it is hard to be good, just as if he had heard him say it is bad to be good. Right, Prodicus?"

"What else do you think Simonides meant, Socrates? He was censuring Pittacus, a man from Lesbos brought up in a barbarous dialect, for not distinguishing words correctly."

"Well, Protagoras, you hear Prodicus. Do you have anything to say in response?"

"You've got it all wrong, Prodicus," Protagoras said. "I am positive that Simonides meant by 'hard' the same thing we do: not 'bad,' but whatever is not easy and takes a lot of effort."

"Oh, but I think so too, Protagoras," I said. "This is what Simonides meant, and Prodicus knows it. He was joking and thought he would test your ability to defend your own statement. The best proof that Simonides did not mean that 'hard' is 'bad' is found in the very next phrase, which says:

God alone can have this privilege.

He cannot very well mean that it is bad to be good if he then says that God alone has this privilege. Prodicus would call Simonides a reprobate for that and no Cean at all. But I would

b

c

d

e

---

49. The Greek *khalepos* means both "difficult" and "bad," as in English, a difficult situation is a bad situation.

50. The Greek term is *deinos*. The adjective form of this word means "awful" in the original sense of "awe-inspiring." The adverbial form, like the English "awfully," was often used simply as an intensifier.

342   like to tell you what I think Simonides' purpose is in this ode, if
       you would like to test my command (to use your term) of po-
       etry. If you'd rather, though, I'll listen to you."
          Protagoras heard me out and said, "If you please, Socrates,"
       and then Prodicus, Hippias, and the others urged me on.
          "All right, then," I said, "I will try to explain to you what I
       think this poem is about. Philosophy, first of all, has its most
       ancient roots and is most widespread among the Greeks in
b   Crete and Lacedaemon, and those regions have the highest con-
       centration of sophists in the world. But the natives deny it and
       pretend to be ignorant in order to conceal the fact that it is by
       their wisdom that they are the leaders of the Greek world,
       something like those sophists Protagoras was talking about.
       Their public image is that they owe their superiority to their
       brave fighting men, and their reason for promoting this image is
       that if the real basis for their superiority were discovered, i.e.
       wisdom, everyone else would start cultivating it. This is top
       secret; not even the Spartanizing cults in the other cities know
       about it, and so you have all these people getting their ears
c   mangled aping the Spartans, lacing on leather gloves, exercising
       fanatically and wearing short capes, as if Sparta's political power
       depended on these things. And when the citizens in Sparta
       want some privacy to have free and open discussions with their
       sophists, they pass alien acts against any Spartanizers and other
       foreigners in town, and conceal their meetings from the rest of
       the world. And so that their young men won't unlearn what
d   they are taught, they do not permit any of them to travel to
       other cities (the Cretans don't either). Crete and Sparta are
       places where there are not only men but women also who take
       pride in their education. You know how to test the truth of my
       contention that the Spartans have the best education in philoso-
       phy and debate? Pick any ordinary Spartan and talk with him
e   for a while. At first you will find he can barely hold up his end
       of the conversation, but at some point he will pick his spot with
       deadly skill and shoot back a terse remark you'll never forget,
       something that will make the person he's talking with (in this
       case you) look like a child. Acute observers have known this for
       a long time now: To be a Spartan is to be a philosopher much
       more than to be an athlete. They know that to be able to say
343   something like that is the mark of a perfectly educated man.
       We're talking about men like Thales of Miletus, Pittacus of
       Mytilene, Bias of Priene, our own Solon, Cleobulus of Lindus,

Myson of Chen, and, the seventh in the list, Chilon of Sparta.[51] All of these emulated, loved, and studied Spartan culture. You can see that distinctive kind of Spartan wisdom in their pithy, memorable sayings, which they jointly dedicated as the first fruits of their wisdom to Apollo in his temple at Delphi, inscribing there the maxims now on everyone's lips: 'Know thyself' and 'Nothing in excess.'[52]

b

"What is my point? That the characteristic style of ancient philosophy was laconic brevity.[53] It was in this context that the saying of Pittacus—*It is hard to be good*—was privately circulated with approval among the sages. Then Simonides, ambitious for philosophical fame, saw that if he could score a takedown against this saying, as if it were a famous wrestler, and get the better of it, he would himself become famous in his own lifetime. So he composed this poem as a deliberate attack against this maxim. That's how it seems to me.

c

"Let's test my hypothesis together, to see whether what I say is true. If all the poet wanted to say was that it is hard to become good, then the beginning of the poem would be crazy, for he inserted there an antithetical particle.[54] It doesn't make any

d

51. Seven Sages of Greece, wise men from sixth and fifth centuries B.C., respected for their practical wisdom. The list of sages varies; others who have been included are Periander of Corinth and Epimenides of Crete.

52. Apollo and the Delphic maxims. Apollo was a complex deity with multiple spheres of power; most relevant in this context were those of prophecy, wisdom, and law. Delphi was the site of the temple to Apollo where it was believed that the god would answer questions put to him through the Pythia (oracular priestess); this temple was also the location of the inscriptions constitutive of the Delphic ethical tradition—*gnōthi seauton* (Know thyself) and *mēden agan* (Nothing in excess).

   Critias refers to the Delphic maxims in Plato's *Charmides* (164c–165b), a dialogue concerned with *sōphrosunē*, the complex virtue which incorporates both maxims. Socrates' interpretation of an oracle from Delphi had a profound effect on his decision to devote his life to philosophizing, according to Plato's account in the *Apology* (20d–23c).

53. Laconia was the name of the outlying area near Sparta and was often used to refer to Sparta; "laconic" is the derived adjective, referring to the linguistic brevity allegedly characteristic of Spartans. Socrates prefers his interlocutors to be laconic.

54. The antithetical particle in question is *men*, which usually sets up a contrast with a following clause marked by the corresponding particle *de*. The *de* clause is not quoted by Plato. An estimated seven lines intervened between the first and second passages quoted by Plato, and these lines have not survived elsewhere, so we do not know what the intended contrast was. The particle *men* is not

sense to insert this unless one supposes that Simonides is addressing the Pittacus maxim as an opponent. Pittacus says it is hard to be good; Simonides rebuts this by saying, 'No, but it is hard for a man to become good, Pittacus, truly.' Notice that he

e does not say truly good; he is not talking about truth in the context of some things being truly good and other things being good but not truly so. This would create an impression of naivete very unlike Simonides. The position of 'truly' in the verse must be a case of hyperbaton.[55] We have to approach this maxim of Pittacus by imagining him speaking and Simonides replying,

344 something like this: Pittacus: 'Gentlemen, it is hard to be good.' Simonides: 'What you say is not true, Pittacus, for it is not being but becoming good, in hands and feet and mind foursquare, blamelessly built—that is hard truly.' This way the insertion of the antithetical particle makes sense, and the 'truly' feels correct in its position at the end. Everything that comes after is evidence for this interpretation. The poem is full of details that

b testify to its excellent composition; indeed, it is a lovely and exquisitely crafted piece, but it would take a long time to go through it from that point of view. Let's review instead the overall structure and intention of the ode, which is from beginning to end a refutation of Pittacus' maxim.

"A few lines later he states (imagine he is making a speech):

c 'To become good truly is hard, and although it may be possible for a short period of time, to persist in that state and to be a good man is, as you say, Pittacus, not humanly possible. God alone can have this privilege,

But that man inevitably is bad
whom incapacitating misfortune throws down.

Whom does incapacitating misfortune throw down when it comes to, say, the command of a ship? Clearly not the ordinary passenger, who is always susceptible. You can't knock down someone already supine; you

translated here because we do not know what shade of contrast was intended and because almost any translation of *men* ("on the one hand," "although") would be too strong. Socrates, in his parody of grammatical exegesis, is deliberately misinterpreting the meaning and force of the particle.

55. Hyperbaton is a figure of speech in which two words that naturally belong together, such as a noun and its adjective, are separated by one or more intervening words. It is fairly common in Greek.

can only knock down someone standing up and render   d
him supine. In the same way, incapacitating misfortune
would overthrow only someone who is capable, not the
chronically incapable. A hurricane striking a pilot would
incapacitate him, a bad season will do it to a farmer, and
the same thing applies to a doctor. For the good is susceptible to becoming bad, as another poet testifies:

The good man is at times bad, at times good.

But the bad is not susceptible to becoming; it must
always be. So that when incapacitating misfortune   e
throws down a man who is capable, wise, and good, he
must inevitably be bad. You say, Pittacus, that it is hard
to be good, that is, to become good is hard, though
possible, but to be good is impossible.

Faring well, every man is good;
Bad, faring ill.

What does it mean to fare well in letters; what makes a
man good at them? Clearly, the learning of letters. What   345
kind of faring well makes a good doctor? Clearly, learning how to cure the sick. 'Bad, faring ill': who could
become a bad doctor? Clearly, someone who is, first, a
doctor and, second, a good doctor. He could in fact
become a bad doctor, but we who are medical laymen
could never by faring ill become doctors or carpenters
or any other kind of professional. And if one cannot   b
become a doctor by faring ill, clearly one cannot become
a bad one either. In the same way a good man may
eventually become bad with the passage of time, or
through hardship, disease, or some other circumstance
that involves the only real kind of faring ill, which is the
loss of knowledge. But the bad man can never become
bad, for he is so all the time. If he is to become bad, he
must first become good. So the tenor of this part of the   c
poem is that it is impossible to be a good man and
continue to be good, but possible for one and the same
person to become good and also bad, and those are best
for the longest time whom the gods love.'

"All this is directed at Pittacus, as the next few lines of the
poem make even clearer:

> *Therefore never shall I seek for the impossible,*
> *cast away my life's lot on empty hope, a quixotic quest*
> *for a blameless man among those who reap*
> *the broad earth's fruit,*

d
> *but if I find him you will have my report.*

This is strong language, and he keeps up his attack on Pittacus' maxim throughout the poem:

> *All who do no wrong[56] willingly*
> *I praise and love.*
> *Necessity not even the gods resist.*

This is spoken to the same end. For Simonides was not so uneducated as to say that he praised all who did nothing bad

e willingly, as if there were anyone who willingly did bad things. I am pretty sure that none of the wise men thinks that any human being willingly makes a mistake or willingly does anything wrong or bad. They know very well that anyone who does anything wrong or bad does so involuntarily. So also Simonides,

346 who does not say that he praises those who willingly do nothing bad; rather he applies the term 'willingly' to himself. He perceived that a good man, an honorable man, often forces himself to love and praise someone utterly different from himself, one's alienated father perhaps, or mother, or country. Scoundrels in a similar situation are almost happy to see their parents' or country's trouble and viciously point it out and denounce it so that their own dereliction of duty toward them will

b not be called into question. They actually exaggerate their complaints and add gratuitous to unavoidable hostility, whereas good men conceal the trouble and force themselves to give praise, and if they are angry because their parents or country wronged them, they calm themselves down and reconcile themselves to it, and they force themselves to love and praise their own people. I think that Simonides reflected that on more than one occasion he himself had eulogized some tyrant or other

c such person, not willingly but because he had to. So he is saying

---

56. The Greek term is *aiskhron*. We have chosen to translate this term variably, in context; the appropriate senses of the term range from base, foul, wretched, contemptible, disgraceful, worthless, reprehensible, vicious, evil, and, as here, wrong. The related term *kakos* we have consistently translated "bad," except at 323d–324b where the neuter plural is translated "evils."

to Pittacus: 'Pittacus, it is not because I am an overcritical person that I am criticizing you, since,

> enough for me a man who is not bad
> nor too intractable, who knows civic Right, a sound man.
> I shall not blame him,
> for I am not fond of blame.
> Infinite the tribe of fools,'

the implication being that a censorious person would have his hands full blaming them.

> 'All is fair in which foul is not mixed.'

The sense here is not that all is white in which black is not mixed, which would be ludicrous in many ways, but rather that he himself accepts without any objection what is in between. 'I do not seek,' he says,   d

> 'for a blameless man among those who reap
> the broad earth's fruit,
> but if I find him you will have my report.'

The meaning is that 'on those terms I will never praise anyone, but I am happy with an average man who does no wrong, since I willingly

> praise and love all'—

—note the Lesbian dialect form of the verb 'praise,'[57] since he is   e
addressing Pittacus—

> 'all who do no wrong'

(this is where the pause should be, before 'willingly')[58]

>   'willingly

> I praise and love

but there are some whom I praise and love unwillingly. So if you spoke something even moderately reasonable and true, Pittacus, I would never censure you. But the fact is that you have   347

---

57. Simonides uses the Aeolic (Lesbian) form of the verb "praise." The significance Socrates attaches to the use of this form is part of the parody.

58. Socrates again is deliberately misconstruing the text when he breaks the line here and takes "willingly" to modify "praise" in the clause that follows when in fact it modifies "do" in the line that precedes.

lied blatantly yet with verisimilitude about extremely important issues, and for that I do censure you.'

"And that, Prodicus and Protagoras," I concluded, "is what I think was going through Simonides' mind when he composed this ode."

Then Hippias said, "I am favorably impressed by your anal-
b   ysis of this ode, Socrates. I have quite a nice talk on it myself, which I will present to you if you wish."

"Yes, Hippias," Alcibiades said, "some other time, though. What should be done now is what Socrates and Protagoras agreed upon, which is for Socrates to answer any questions Protagoras may still have to ask, or if he so chooses, to answer Socrates' questions."

c   Then I said, "I leave it up to Protagoras, but if it's all right with him, why don't we say good-bye to odes and poetry and get back to what I first asked him, a question, Protagoras, which I would be glad to settle in a joint investigation with you. Discussing poetry strikes me as no different from the second-rate drinking parties of the agora crowd. These people, largely un-educated and unable to entertain themselves over their wine by
d   using their own voices to generate conversation, pay premium prices for flute-girls and rely on the extraneous voice of the reed flute as background music for their parties. But when well-educated gentlemen drink together, you will not see girls play-ing the flute or the lyre or dancing, but a group that knows how to get together without these childish frivolities, conversing
e   civilly no matter how heavily they are drinking. Ours is such a group, if indeed it consists of men such as most of us claim to be, and it should require no extraneous voices, not even of po-ets, who cannot be questioned on what they say. When a poet is brought up in a discussion, almost everyone has a different opinion about what he means, and they wind up arguing about something they can never finally decide. The best people avoid
348 such discussions and rely on their own powers of speech to entertain themselves and test each other. These people should be our models. We should put the poets aside and converse directly with each other, testing the truth and our own ideas. If you have more questions to ask, I am ready to answer them; or, if you prefer, you can render the same service to me, and we can resume where we broke off and try to reach a conclusion."

b   I went on in this vein, but Protagoras would not state clearly which alternative he preferred. So Alcibiades looked over at

Callias and said, "Callias, do you think Protagoras is behaving well in not making it clear whether he will participate in the discussion or not? I certainly don't. He should either participate or say he is not going to, so we will know how he stands, and Socrates, or whoever, can start a discussion with someone else."

It looked to me that Protagoras was embarrassed by Al-   c
cibiades' words, not to mention the insistence of Callias and practically the whole company. In the end he reluctantly brought himself to resume our dialogue and indicated he was ready to be asked questions.

"Protagoras," I said, "I don't want you to think that my motive in talking with you is anything else than to take a good hard look at things that continually perplex me. I think that Homer said it all in the line,

Going in tandem, one perceives before the other.[59]   d

Human beings are simply more resourceful this way in action, speech, and thought. If someone has a private perception, he immediately starts going around and looking until he finds somebody he can show it to and have it corroborated. And there is a particular reason why I would rather talk with you than anyone else: I think you are the best qualified to investigate the sort of things that decent and respectable individuals ought to   e
examine, and virtue especially. Who else but you? Not only do you consider yourself to be noble and good but, unlike others who are themselves decent and respectable individuals yet unable to make others so, you are not only good yourself but able to make others good as well, and you have so much self-confidence that instead of concealing this skill, as others do, you advertise it openly to the whole Greek world, calling yourself a   349
sophist, highlighting yourself as a teacher of virtue, the first ever to have deemed it appropriate to charge a fee for this. How could I not solicit your help in a joint investigation of these questions? There is no way I could not.

"So right now I want you to remind me of some of the questions I first asked, starting from the beginning. Then I want to proceed together to take a good hard look at some other ques-   b
tions. I believe the first question was this: Wisdom, temperance, courage, justice, and piety—are these five names for the same thing, or is there underlying each of these names a unique

59. Homer, *Iliad* 10.224.

thing, a thing with its own power or function, each one unlike any of the others? You said that they are not names for the same
c thing, that each of these names refers to a unique thing, and that all these are parts of virtue, not like the parts of gold, which are similar to each other and to the whole of which they are parts, but like the parts of a face, dissimilar to the whole of which they are parts and to each other, and each one having its own unique power or function. If this is still your view, say so; if it's changed in any way, make your new position clear, for I am certainly not going to hold you accountable for what you said
d before if you want to say something at all different now. In fact, I wouldn't be surprised if you were just trying out something on me before."

"What I am saying to you, Socrates, is that all these are parts of virtue, and that while four of them are reasonably close to each other, courage is completely different from all the rest. The proof that what I am saying is true is that you will find many people who are extremely unjust, impious, intemperate, and ignorant, and yet exceptionally courageous."

e "Hold it right there," I said. "This is worth looking into. Would you say courageous men are confident, or something else?"

"Confident, yes, and ready for action where most men would be afraid."

"Well, then, do you agree that virtue is something fine, and that you offer yourself as a teacher of it because it is fine?"

"The finest thing of all, unless I am quite out of my mind."

"Then is part of it worthless and part of it fine, or all of it fine?"

"Surely it is all as fine as can be."

350 "Do you know who dives confidently into wells?"

"Of course, divers."

"Is this because they know what they are doing, or for some other reason?"

"Because they know what they are doing."

"Who are confident in fighting from horseback? Riders or nonriders?"

"Riders."

"And in fighting with shields? Shieldmen or nonshieldmen?"

"Shieldmen, and so on down the line, if that's what you're getting at. Those with the right kind of knowledge are always more confident than those without it, and a given individual is more confident after he acquires it than he was before."

"But haven't you ever seen men lacking knowledge of all of these occupations yet confident in each of them?"   b

"I have, all too confident."

"Is their confidence courage?"

"No, because courage would then be contemptible. These men are out of their minds."

"Then what do you mean by courageous men? Aren't they those who are confident?"

"I still hold by that."   c

"Then these men who are so confident turn out to be not courageous but mad? And, on the other side, the wisest are the most confident and the most confident are the most courageous? And the logical conclusion would be that wisdom is courage?"

"You are doing a poor job of remembering what I said when I answered your questions, Socrates. When I was asked if the courageous are confident, I agreed. I was not asked if the confident are courageous. If you had asked me that, I would have said, 'Not all of them.' You have nowhere shown that my assent   d
to the proposition that the courageous are confident was in error. What you did show next was that knowledge increases one's confidence and makes one more confident than those without knowledge. In consequence of this you conclude that courage and wisdom are the same thing. But by following this line of reasoning you could conclude that strength and wisdom are the same thing. First you would ask me if the strong are powerful, and I would say yes. Then, if those who know how to   e
wrestle are more powerful than those who do not, and if individual wrestlers became more powerful after they learn than they were before. Again I would say yes. After I had agreed to these things, it would be open to you to use precisely these points of agreement to prove that wisdom is strength. But nowhere in this process do I agree that the powerful are strong, only that the strong are powerful. Strength and power[60] are not   351
the same thing. Power derives from knowledge and also from passionate emotion. Strength comes from nature and proper nurture of the body. So also confidence and courage are not the

---

60. Here, *dunami*s is best translated in perhaps its most literal sense—power.

same thing, with the consequence that the courageous are confident, but not all those who are confident are courageous. For
confidence, like power, comes from skill (and from passionate
emotion as well); courage, from nature and the proper nurture
of the soul."

b   "Would you say, Protagoras, that some people live well and
others live badly?"

"Yes."

"But does it seem to you that a person lives well, if he lives
distressed and in pain?"

"No, indeed."

"Now, if he completed his life, having lived pleasantly, does
he not seem to you to have lived well?"

"It seems that way to me."

c   "So, then, to live pleasantly is good, and unpleasantly, bad?"

"Yes, so long as he lived having taken pleasure in honorable
things."

"What, Protagoras? Surely you don't, like most people, call
some pleasant things bad and some painful things good? I
mean, isn't a pleasant thing good just insofar as it is pleasant,
that is, if it results in nothing other than pleasure; and, on the
other hand, aren't painful things bad in the same way, just insofar as they are painful?"

"I don't know, Socrates, if I should answer as simply as you
d   put the question—that everything pleasant is good and everything painful is bad. It seems to me to be safer to respond not
merely with my present answer in mind but from the point of
view of my life overall, that on the one hand, there are pleasurable things which are not good, and on the other hand, there
are painful things which are not bad but some which are, and a
third class which is neutral—neither bad nor good."

e   "You call pleasant things those which partake of pleasure or
produce pleasure?"

"Certainly."

"So my question is this: Just insofar as things are pleasurable
are they good? I am asking whether pleasure itself is not a
good."

"Just as you always say, Socrates, let us inquire into this matter, and if your claim seems reasonable and it is established that
pleasure and the good are the same, then we will come to agreement; otherwise we will disagree."

"Do you wish to lead this inquiry, or shall I?"

"It is fitting for you to lead, for it is you who brought up the idea."

"All right, will this help to make it clear? When someone   352
evaluates a man's health or other functions of the body through his appearance, he looks at the face and extremities, and might say: 'Show me your chest and back too, so that I can make a better examination.' That's the kind of investigation I want to make. Having seen how you stand on the good and the pleasant, I need to say something like this to you: Come now, Protagoras, and reveal this about your mind: What do you think   b about knowledge? Do you go along with the majority or not? Most people think this way about it, that it is not a powerful thing, neither a leader nor a ruler. They do not think of it in that way at all; but rather in this way: while knowledge is often present in a man, what rules him is not knowledge but rather anything else—sometimes desire, sometimes pleasure, sometimes pain, at other times love, often fear; they think of his knowledge as being utterly dragged around by all these other   c things as if it were a slave. Now, does the matter seem like that to you, or does it seem to you that knowledge is a fine thing capable of ruling a person, and if someone were to know what is good and bad, then he would not be forced by anything to act otherwise than knowledge dictates, and intelligence would be sufficient to save a person?"

"Not only does it seem just as you say, Socrates, but further, it would be shameful indeed for me above all people to say that wisdom and knowledge are anything but the most powerful   d forces in human activity."

"Right you are. You realize that most people aren't going to be convinced by us. They maintain that most people are unwilling to do what is best, even though they know what it is and are able to do it. And when I have asked them the reason for this, they say that those who act that way do so because they are overcome by pleasure or pain or are being ruled by one of the things I referred   e to just now."

"I think people say a lot of other things erroneously too, Socrates."

"Come with me, then, and let's try to persuade people and to teach them what is this experience which they call being over-   353 come by pleasure, because of which they fail to do the best thing when they know what it is. For perhaps if we told them that what they were saying isn't true, but is demonstrably false, they would ask us: 'Protagoras and Socrates, if this is not the experience of being overcome by pleasure, but something other than that, what do you two say it is? Tell us.'"

"Socrates, why is it necessary for us to investigate the opinion of ordinary people, who will say whatever occurs to them?"

b   "I think this will help us find out about courage, how it is related to the other parts of virtue. If you are willing to go along with what we agreed just now, that I will lead us toward what I think will turn out to be the best way to make things clear, then fine; if you are not willing, I will give it up."

"No, you are right; proceed as you have begun."

c   "Going back, then; if they should ask us: 'We have been speaking of "being overcome by pleasure". What do you say this is?' I would reply to them this way: 'Listen. Protagoras and I will try to explain it to you. Do you say, gentlemen, this happens to you in circumstances like these—you are often overcome by pleasant things like food or drink or sex, and you do those things all the while knowing they are ruinous?' They would say yes. Then you and I would ask them again: 'In what sense do

d   you call these things ruinous? Is it that each of them is pleasant in itself and produces immediate pleasure, or is it that later they bring about diseases and poverty and many other things of that sort? Or even if it doesn't bring about these things later, but gives only enjoyment, would it still be a bad thing, just because it gives enjoyment in whatever way?' Can we suppose then, Protagoras, that they would make any other answer than that bad things are bad not because they bring about immediate pleasure, but rather because of what happens later, disease and things like that?'"

e   "I think that is how most people would answer."

"'And in bringing about diseases and poverty, do they bring about pain?' I think they would agree."

"Yes."

"'Does it not seem to you, my good people, as Protagoras and I maintain, that these things are bad on account of nothing

354 other than the fact that they result in pain and deprive us of other pleasures?' Would they agree?"

Protagoras concurred.

"Then again, suppose we were to ask them the opposite question: 'You who say that some painful things are good, do you not say that such things as athletics and military training and treatments by doctors such as cautery, surgery, medicines, and

starvation diet are good things even though painful?' Would
they say so?"

"Yes."

" 'Would you call these things good for the reason that they   b
bring about intense pain and suffering, or because they ultimately bring about health and good condition of bodies and pres-
ervation of cities and power over others and wealth?' Would they
agree?"

"Yes."

"These things are good because they result in pleasure and in
the relief and avoidance of pain? 'Or do you have some other criterion in view, other than pleasure and pain, on the basis of
which you would call these things good?' They would say no, I
think."   c

"And I would agree with you."

" 'So then you pursue pleasure as being good, and avoid pain
as bad?' "

"Yes."

" 'So, this you regard as bad, pain, and pleasure you regard as
good, since you call the very enjoying of something bad whenever it deprives us of greater pleasures than it itself provides, or
brings about greater pains than the very pleasures inherent in   d
it? But if you call the very enjoying of something bad, for some
other reason and with some other criterion in view than the one
I have suggested, you could tell us what it is; but you won't be
able to.' "

"I don't think they'll be able to either."

" 'And likewise concerning the actual state of being in pain? Do
you call the actual condition of being in pain good, whenever it
relieves pains greater than the ones it contains or brings about
greater pleasures than its attendant pains? Now, if you are using   e
some other criterion than the one I have suggested, when you call
the very condition of being pained good, you can tell us what it is;
but you won't be able to do so.' "

"Truly spoken."

"Now, again, gentlemen, if you asked me: 'Why are you going
on so much about this and in so much detail?' I would reply,
forgive me. First of all, it is not easy to show what it is that you
call 'being overcome by pleasure,' and then, it is upon this very
point that all the arguments rest. But even now it is still possi-   355
ble to withdraw, if you are able to say that the good is anything
other than pleasure or that the bad is anything other than pain,

or is it enough for you to live life pleasantly without pain? If it is enough, and you are not able to say anything else than that the good and the bad are that which result in pleasure and pain, listen to this. For I say to you that if this is so, your position will become absurd, when you say that frequently a man, knowing

b   the bad to be bad, nevertheless does that very thing, when he is able not to do it, having been driven and overwhelmed by pleasure; and again when you say that a man knowing the good is not willing to do it, on account of immediate pleasure, having been overcome by it. Just how absurd this is will become very clear, if we do not use so many names at the same time, 'pleasant' and 'painful,' 'good' and 'bad'; but since these turned out to be only two things, let us instead agree on two names, first,

c   'good' and 'bad,' then later, 'pleasant' and 'painful.' On that basis, then, let us say that a man knowing bad things to be bad, does them all the same. If then someone asks us: 'Why?' 'Having been overcome,' we shall reply. 'By what?' he will ask us. We are no longer able to say 'by pleasure,'—for it has taken on its other name, 'the good' instead of 'pleasure'—so we will say and reply that 'he is overcome'. . . 'By what?' he will ask. 'By the good,' we will say, 'for heaven's sake.' If by chance the

d   questioner is rude, he might burst out laughing and say: 'What you're saying is ridiculous—someone does what is bad, knowing that it is bad, when it is not being necessary to do it having been overcome by the good. So,' he will say, 'within yourself, does the good outweigh the bad or not?' We will clearly say in reply that it does not; for if it did, the person whom we say is overcome by pleasure would not have made any mistakes. 'In virtue of what,' he might say, 'does the good *outweigh* the bad or

e   the bad the good? Only in that one is greater and one is smaller, or more and less.' We could not help but agree. 'So clearly then,' he will say, 'by "being overcome" you mean getting more bad things for the sake of fewer good things.'[61] That settles that, then.

   "So let's now go back and apply the names 'the pleasant' and 'the painful' to these very same things. Now let us say that a man does what before we called 'bad things' and now shall call 'pain-

---

61. This translation construes the Greek preposition *anti* as meaning "for the sake of" (s.v. *anti*, Liddell & Scott and Plato, *Menexenus* 237a). The verb *lambanein* is translated as "get" in order to capture the twofold meaning of the verb in Greek: "to take" and "to receive."

ful' ones, knowing they are painful, but being overcome by pleasant things, although it is clear that they do not outweigh them.
But how else does pleasure outweigh pain, except in relative excess or deficiency? Isn't it a matter (to use other terms) of larger
and smaller, more or fewer, greater or lesser degree?

"For if someone were to say: 'But Socrates, the immediate
pleasure is very much different from the pleasant and the painful at a later time,' I would reply, 'They are not different in any
other way than by pleasure and pain, for there is no other way   b
that they could differ. Weighing is a good analogy; you put the
pleasures together and the pains together, both the near and the
remote, on the balance scale, and then say which of the two is
more. For if you weigh pleasant things against pleasant, the
greater and the more must always be taken; if painful things
against painful, the fewer and the smaller. And if you weigh
pleasant things against painful, and if the painful is exceeded by
the pleasant—whether the near by the remote or the remote by
the near—you have to perform that action in which the pleasant
prevails; on the other hand, if the pleasant is exceeded by the   c
painful, you have to refrain from doing that. Does it seem any
different to you, my friends?' I know that they would not say
otherwise."

Protagoras assented.

"Since this is so, I will say to them: 'Answer me this: Do things
of the same size appear to you larger when seen near at hand and
smaller when seen from a distance, or not?' They would say they
do. 'And similarly for thickness and pluralities? And equal sounds
seem louder when near at hand, softer when farther away?' They
would agree. 'If then our well-being depended upon this, doing   d
and choosing large things avoiding and not doing the small ones,
what would we see as our salvation in life? Would it be the art of
measurement or the power of appearance? While the power of appearance often makes us wander all over the place in confusion,
often changing our minds about the same things and regretting
our actions and choices with respect to things large and small, the
art of measurement, in contrast, would make the appearances lose   e
their power by showing us the truth, would give us peace of mind
firmly rooted in the truth and would save our life.' Therefore,
would these men agree, with this in mind, that the art of measurement would save us, or some other art?"

"I agree, the art of measurement would."

"What if our salvation in life depended on our choices of odd and even, when the greater and the lesser had to be counted correctly, either the same kind against itself or one kind against the other, whether it be near or remote? What then would save our life? Surely nothing other than knowledge, specifically some kind of measurement, since that is the art of the greater and the lesser? In fact, nothing other than arithmetic, since it's a question of the odd and even? Would most people agree with us or not?"

Protagoras thought they would agree.

"Well, then, my good people: Since it has turned out that our salvation in life depends on the right choice of pleasures and pains, be they more or fewer, greater or lesser, farther or nearer, doesn't our salvation seem, first of all, to be measurement, which is the study of relative excess and deficiency and equality?"

"It must be."

"And since it is measurement, it must definitely be an art, and knowledge."

"They will agree."

"What exactly this art, this knowledge is, we can inquire into later; that it is knowledge of some sort is enough for the demonstration which Protagoras and I have to give in order to answer the question which you asked us. You asked it, if you remember, when we were agreeing that nothing was stronger or better than knowledge, which always prevails, whenever it is present, over pleasure and everything else. At that point you said that pleasure often rules even the man who knows; since we disagreed, you went on to ask us this: 'Protagoras and Socrates, if this experience is not being overcome by pleasure, what is it then; what do you say it is? Tell us.' 'If immediately we had said to you "ignorance," you might have laughed at us, but if you laugh at us now, you will be laughing at yourselves. For you agreed with us that those who make mistakes with regard to the choice of pleasure and pain, in other words, with regard to good and bad, do so because of a lack of knowledge, and that it was not merely a lack of knowledge but a lack of that knowledge you agreed was measurement. And the mistaken act done without knowledge you must know is one done from ignorance. So this is what "being overcome by pleasure" is—ignorance in the highest degree, and it is this which Protagoras and Prodicus and Hippias claim to cure. But you, thinking it to be something other than ignorance, do not yourselves go to sophists, nor do you send your children to them for instruction, believing as you do that we are dealing with someone unteachable. By worrying about your money and not giving it to them, you all do badly in both private and public life.'

"This is how we would have answered the many. Now, I ask you, Hippias and Prodicus, as well as Protagoras—this is your conversation also—to say whether you think what I say is true or false." They all thought that what I said was marvelously true.

"So you agree, that the pleasant is good, the painful bad. I beg indulgence of Prodicus who distinguishes among words; for whether you call it 'pleasant' or 'delightful' or 'enjoyable,' or whatever way or manner you please to name this sort of thing, my excellent Prodicus, please respond to the intent of my question." Prodicus, laughing, agreed, as did the others.

"Well, then, men, what about this? Are not all actions leading toward living painlessly and pleasantly honorable and beneficial? And isn't honorable activity good and beneficial?"

They agreed.

"Then if the pleasant is the good, no one who knows or believes there is something else better than what he is doing, something possible, will go on doing what he had been doing when he could be doing what is better. To give in to oneself is nothing other than ignorance, and to control oneself is nothing other than wisdom."

They all agreed.

"Well, then, do you say that ignorance is to have a false belief and to be deceived about matters of importance?"

They all agreed on this.

"Now, no one goes willingly toward the bad or what he believes to be bad; neither is it in human nature, so it seems, to want to go toward what one believes to be bad instead of to the good. And when he is forced to choose between one of two bad things, no one will choose the greater if he is able to choose the lesser."

They agreed with all of that too.

"Well, then, is there something you call dread or fear? And I address this to you, Prodicus. I say that whether you call it fear or dread, it is an expectation of something bad."

Protagoras and Hippias thought that this was true of both

358

b

c

d

e   dread and fear, but Prodicus thought it applied to dread, but not
        to fear.
        "Well, it does not really matter, Prodicus. This is the point. If
        what I have said up to now is true, then would anyone be
        willing to go toward what he dreads, when he can go toward
        what he does not? Or is this impossible from what we have
        agreed? For it was agreed that what one fears one holds to be
        bad; no one goes toward those things which he holds to be bad,
        or chooses those things willingly."
359   They all agreed.
        "Well, Prodicus and Hippias, with this established, let Pro-
        tagoras defend for us the truth of his first answer. I don't mean
        his very first answer, for then he said that while there are five
        parts of virtue, none is like any other, but each one has its own
        unique power or function. I'm not talking about this now, but
b   about what he said later. For later he said that four of them are
        very similar to each other, but that one differs very much from
        the others, that one being courage. And he said that I would
        know this by the following evidence: 'You will find, Socrates,
        many people who are extremely impious, unjust, intemperate,
        and ignorant, and yet exceptionally courageous; by this you will
        recognize that courage differs very much from all the other
        parts of virtue.' I was very surprised at his answer then, and
        even more so now that I have gone over these things with you. I
        asked him then if he said that the courageous were confident.
c   And he said, 'Yes, and ready for action too.' Do you remember
        giving this answer?"
        He said he did.
        "Well, then, tell us, for what actions are the courageous
        ready? The same actions as the cowardly?"
        "No."
        "Different actions?"
        "Yes."
        "Do the cowardly go forward to things which are easily ven-
        tured, and the courageous toward things to be feared?"
        "So it is said by most people."
d   "Right, but I am not asking that. Rather, what do *you* say the
        courageous go toward with daring: toward things to be feared,
        believing them to be fearsome, or toward things not to be
        feared?"
        "By what you have just said, the former is impossible."

"Right again; so, if our demonstration has been correct, then no one goes toward those things he considers to be fearsome, since not to be in control of oneself was found to be ignorance."

He agreed.

"But all people, both the courageous and the cowardly, go toward that about which they are confident; both the cowardly   e
and the courageous go toward the same things."

"But, Socrates, what the cowardly go toward is completely opposite to what the courageous go toward. For example, the courageous are willing to go to war, but the cowardly are not."

"Is going to war honorable or is it disgraceful?"

"Honorable."

"Then, if it is honorable, we have agreed before, it is also good, for we agreed that all honorable actions were good."

"Very true, and I always believed this."

"And rightly; but who would you say are not willing to go to   360
war, war being honorable and good?"

"The cowardly."

"If a thing is noble and good, is it also pleasant?"

"That was definitely agreed upon."

"So, the cowardly, with full knowledge, are not willing to go toward the more honorable, the better, and more pleasant?"

"If we agree to that, we will undermine what we agreed on earlier."

"What about the courageous man: Does he go toward the more honorable, the better, and more pleasant?"

"We must agree to that."

"So, generally, when the courageous fear, their fear is not disgraceful; nor when they are confident is their confidence disgraceful."

"True."   b

"If not disgraceful, is it honorable?"

He agreed.

"If honorable, then also good?"

"Yes."

"Whereas the fear and confidence of the cowardly, the foolhardy, and madmen are disgraceful?"

He agreed.

"Is their confidence disgraceful and bad for any reason other than ignorance and stupidity?"

"No, it isn't."   c

"Now then; that through which cowardly people are cowardly, do you call it cowardice or courage?"

"Cowardice."

"And aren't cowards shown to be so through their ignorance of what is to be feared?"

"Absolutely."

"So they are cowards because of that ignorance?"

He agreed.

"You agreed that it is through cowardice that they are cowards?"

He said he did.

"So, can we conclude that cowardice is ignorance of what is and is not to be feared?"

He nodded.

d   "Now, courage is the opposite of cowardice."

He said yes.

"So then, wisdom about what is and is not to be feared is the opposite of this ignorance?"

He nodded again.

"And this ignorance is cowardice?"

He nodded again, very reluctantly.

"So the wisdom about what is and is not to be feared is courage and is the opposite of this ignorance?"

He would not even nod at this; he remained silent.

And I said, "What's this, Protagoras? Will you not say yes or no to my question?"

"Answer it yourself."

e   "I have only one more question to ask you. Do you still believe, as you did at first, that some men are extremely ignorant and yet still very courageous?"

"I think that you just want to win the argument, Socrates, and that is why you are forcing me to answer. So I will gratify you and say that, on the basis of what we have agreed upon, it seems to me to be impossible."

"I have no other reason for asking these things than my desire to answer these questions about virtue, especially what virtue is in itself. For I know that if we could get clear on that, then we would be able to settle the question about which we both have had much to say, I—that virtue cannot be taught, you—that it can.

"It seems to me that our discussion has turned on us, and if it had a voice of its own, it would say, mockingly, 'Socrates and

Protagoras, how ridiculous you are, both of you. Socrates, you said earlier that virtue cannot be taught, but now you are argu- b ing the very opposite and have attempted to show that every- thing is knowledge—justice, temperance, courage—in which case, virtue would appear to be eminently teachable. On the other hand, if virtue is anything other than knowledge, as Pro- tagoras has been trying to say, then it would clearly be unteach- able. But, if it turns out to be wholly knowledge, as you now urge, Socrates, it would be very surprising indeed if virtue could not be taught. Now, Protagoras maintained at first that it could be taught, but now he thinks the opposite, urging that hardly c any of the virtues turn out to be knowledge. On that view, virtue could hardly be taught at all.'

"Now, Protagoras, seeing that we have gotten this topsy-turvy and terribly confused, I am most eager to clear it all up, and I would like us, having come this far, to continue until we come d through to what virtue is in itself, and then to return to inquire about whether it can or cannot be taught, so that Epimetheus might not frustrate us a second time in this inquiry, as he ne- glected us in the distribution of powers and abilities in your story. I liked the Prometheus character in your story better than Epimetheus. Since I take promethean forethought over my life as a whole, I pay attention to these things, and if you are will- ing, as I said at the beginning, I would be pleased to investigate them along with you."

"Socrates, I commend your enthusiasm and the way you find your way through an argument. I really don't think I am a bad man, certainly the last man to harbor ill will. Indeed, I have told e many people that I admire you more than anyone I have met, certainly more than anyone in your generation. And I say that I would not be surprised if you gain among men high repute for wisdom. We will examine these things later, whenever you wish; now it is time to turn our attention elsewhere."

"That is what we should do, if it seems right to you. It is long 362 since time for me to keep that appointment I mentioned. I stayed only as a favor to our noble colleague Callias."

Our conversation was over, and so we left.